DATE DUE			
MR 07 '90	AG 23 '96		
AP 13 '90	MAR 3 1 2000		
FE 2 '91	PR 18		
NO 27 '91			
Dec 9			
JA 25 '92			
SE 09 '94			
JA 23 '95			
DE 26 '95			
JA 24 '96			

Simmons, William S

The Narragansett

THE
NARRAGANSETT

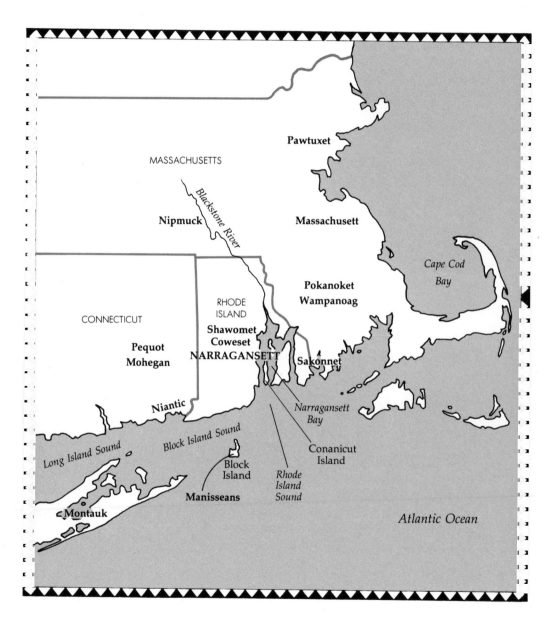

MASSACHUSETTS

Pawtuxet

Nipmuck

Blackstone River

Massachusett

RHODE ISLAND

CONNECTICUT

Cape Cod Bay

Pokanoket Wampanoag

Shawomet Coweset NARRAGANSETT

Pequot Mohegan

Sakonnet

Niantic

Narragansett Bay

Conanicut Island

Long Island Sound

Block Island Sound

Block Island

Rhode Island Sound

Manisseans

Montauk

Atlantic Ocean

INDIANS OF NORTH AMERICA

THE
NARRAGANSETT

William S. Simmons
University of California at Berkeley

Frank W. Porter III
General Editor

CHELSEA HOUSE PUBLISHERS
New York Philadelphia

On the cover Bola tie of glass beads, made by Len Bayrd, Narragansett

Chelsea House Publishers
Editor-in-Chief Nancy Toff
Executive Editor Remmel T. Nunn
Managing Editor Karyn Gullen Browne
Copy Chief Juliann Barbato
Picture Editor Adrian G. Allen
Art Director Maria Epes
Manufacturing Manager Gerald Levine

Indians of North America
Senior Editor Marjorie P. K. Weiser

Staff for **THE NARRAGANSETT**
Deputy Copy Chief Ellen Scordato
Editorial Assistant Claire M. Wilson
Assistant Art Director Laurie Jewell
Designer Donna Sinisgalli
Design Assistant James Baker
Picture Researcher Kim Dramer
Production Coordinator Joseph Romano

First Printing

1 3 5 7 9 8 6 4 2

Library of Congress Cataloging-in-Publication Data

Simmons, William Scranton, 1938–
The Narragansett / William S. Simmons.
p.   cm.—(Indians of North America)
Bibliography: p.
Includes index.
Summary: Examines the history, culture, and changing
fortunes of the Narragansett Indians of Rhode Island.
ISBN 1-55546-718-0
      0-7910-0364-7 (pbk.)
1. Narragansett Indians. [1. Narragansett Indians. 2. Indians
of North America.] I. Title. II. Series: Indians of North
America (Chelsea House Publishers)
E99.N16S52   1989   88-28323
973'.0497—dc 19   CIP

CONTENTS

INDIANS OF NORTH AMERICA

CHELSEA HOUSE PUBLISHERS

INDIANS OF NORTH AMERICA: CONFLICT AND SURVIVAL

Frank W. Porter III

The Indians survived our open intention of wiping them out, and since the tide turned they have even weathered our good intentions toward them, which can be much more deadly.

John Steinbeck
America and Americans

When Europeans first reached the North American continent, they found hundreds of tribes occupying a vast and rich country. The newcomers quickly recognized the wealth of natural resources. They were not, however, so quick or willing to recognize the spiritual, cultural, and intellectual riches of the people they called Indians.

The Indians of North America examines the problems that develop when people with different cultures come together. For American Indians, the consequences of their interaction with non-Indian people have been both productive and tragic. The Europeans believed they had "discovered" a "New World," but their religious bigotry, cultural bias, and materialistic world view kept them from appreciating and understanding the people who lived in it. All too often they attempted to change the way of life of the indigenous people. The Spanish conquistadores wanted the Indians as a source of labor. The Christian missionaries, many of whom were English, viewed them as potential converts. French traders and trappers used the Indians as a means to obtain pelts. As Francis Parkman, the 19th-century historian, stated, "Spanish civilization crushed the Indian; English civilization scorned and neglected him; French civilization embraced and cherished him."

Nearly 500 years later, many people think of American Indians as curious vestiges of a distant past, waging a futile war to survive in a Space Age society. Even today, our understanding of the history and culture of American Indians is too often derived from unsympathetic, culturally biased, and inaccurate reports. The American Indian, described and portrayed in thousands of movies, television programs, books, articles, and government studies, has either been raised to the status of the "noble savage" or disparaged as the "wild Indian" who resisted the westward expansion of the American frontier.

7

Where in this popular view are the real Indians, the human beings and communities whose ancestors can be traced back to ice-age hunters? Where are the creative and indomitable people whose sophisticated technologies used the natural resources to ensure their survival, whose military skill might even have prevented European settlement of North America if not for devastating epidemics and the disruption of the ecology? Where are the men and women who are today diligently struggling to assert their legal rights and express once again the value of their heritage?

The various Indian tribes of North America, like people everywhere, have a history that includes population expansion, adaptation to a range of regional environments, trade across wide networks, internal strife, and warfare. This was the reality. Europeans justified their conquests, however, by creating a mythical image of the New World and its native people. In this myth, the New World was a virgin land, waiting for the Europeans. The arrival of Christopher Columbus ended a timeless primitiveness for the original inhabitants.

Also part of this myth was the debate over the origins of the American Indians. Fantastic and diverse answers were proposed by the early explorers, missionaries, and settlers. Some thought that the Indians were descended from the Ten Lost Tribes of Israel, others that they were descended from inhabitants of the lost continent of Atlantis. One writer suggested that the Indians had reached North America in another Noah's ark.

A later myth, perpetrated by many historians, focused on the relentless persecution during the past five centuries until only a scattering of these "primitive" people remained to be herded onto reservations. This view fails to chronicle the overt and covert ways in which the Indians successfully coped with the intruders.

All of these myths presented one-sided interpretations that ignored the complexity of European and American events and policies. All left serious questions unanswered. What were the origins of the American Indians? Where did they come from? How and when did they get to the New World? What was their life—their culture—really like?

In the late 1800s, anthropologists and archaeologists in the Smithsonian Institution's newly created Bureau of American Ethnology in Washington, D. C., began to study scientifically the history and culture of the Indians of North America. They were motivated by an honest belief that the Indians were on the verge of extinction and that along with them would vanish their languages, religious beliefs, technology, myths, and legends. These men and women went out to visit, study, and record data from as many Indian communities as possible before this information was forever lost.

By this time there was a new myth in the national consciousness. American Indians existed as figures in the American past. They had performed a historical mission. They had challenged white settlers who trekked across the continent. Once conquered, however, they were supposed to accept graciously the way of life of their conquerors.

The reality again was different. American Indians resisted both actively and passively. They refused to lose their unique identity, to be assimilated into white society. Many whites viewed the Indians not only as members of a conquered nation but also as "inferior" and "unequal." The rights of the Indians could be expanded, contracted, or modified as the conquerors saw fit. In every generation, white society asked itself what to do with the American Indians. Their answers have resulted in the twists and turns of federal Indian policy.

There were two general approaches. One way was to raise the Indians to a "higher level" by "civilizing" them. Zealous missionaries considered it their Christian duty to elevate the Indian through conversion and scanty education. The other approach was to ignore the Indians until they disappeared under pressure from the ever-expanding white society. The myth of the "vanishing Indian" gave stronger support to the latter option, helping to justify the taking of the Indians' land.

Prior to the end of the 18th century, there was no national policy on Indians simply because the American nation had not yet come into existence. American Indians similarly did not possess a political or social unity with which to confront the various Europeans. They were not homogeneous. Rather, they were loosely formed bands and tribes, speaking nearly 300 languages and thousands of dialects. The collective identity felt by Indians today is a result of their common experiences of defeat and/or mistreatment at the hands of whites.

During the colonial period, the British crown did not have a coordinated policy toward the Indians of North America. Specific tribes (most notably the Iroquois and the Cherokee) became military and political pawns used by both the crown and the individual colonies. The success of the American Revolution brought no immediate change. When the United States acquired new territory from France and Mexico in the early 19th century, the federal government wanted to open this land to settlement by homesteaders. But the Indian tribes that lived on this land had signed treaties with European governments assuring their title to the land. Now the United States assumed legal responsibility for honoring these treaties.

At first, President Thomas Jefferson believed that the Louisiana Purchase contained sufficient land for both the Indians and the white population.

Within a generation, though, it became clear that the Indians would not be allowed to remain. In the 1830s the federal government began to coerce the eastern tribes to sign treaties agreeing to relinquish their ancestral land and move west of the Mississippi River. Whenever these negotiations failed, President Andrew Jackson used the military to remove the Indians. The southeastern tribes, promised food and transportation during their removal to the West, were instead forced to walk the "Trail of Tears." More than 4,000 men, women, and children died during this forced march. The "removal policy" was successful in opening the land to homesteaders, but it created enormous hardships for the Indians.

By 1871 most of the tribes in the United States had signed treaties ceding most or all of their ancestral land in exchange for reservations and welfare. The treaty terms were intended to bind both parties for all time. But in the General Allotment Act of 1887, the federal government changed its policy again. Now the goal was to make tribal members into individual landowners and farmers, encouraging their absorption into white society. This policy was advantageous to whites who were eager to acquire Indian land, but it proved disastrous for the Indians. One hundred thirty-eight million acres of reservation land were subdivided into tracts of 160, 80, or as little as 40 acres, and allotted to tribe members on an individual basis. Land owned in this way was said to have "trust status" and could not be sold. But the surplus land—all Indian land not allotted to individuals— was opened (for sale) to white settlers. Ultimately, more than 90 million acres of land were taken from the Indians by legal and illegal means.

The resulting loss of land was a catastrophe for the Indians. It was necessary to make it illegal for Indians to sell their land to non-Indians. The Indian Reorganization Act of 1934 officially ended the allotment period. Tribes that voted to accept the provisions of this act were reorganized, and an effort was made to purchase land within preexisting reservations to restore an adequate land base.

Ten years later, in 1944, federal Indian policy again shifted. Now the federal government wanted to get out of the "Indian business." In 1953 an act of Congress named specific tribes whose trust status was to be ended "at the earliest possible time." This new law enabled the United States to end unilaterally, whether the Indians wished it or not, the special status that protected the land in Indian tribal reservations. In the 1950s federal Indian policy was to transfer federal responsibility and jurisdiction to state governments, encourage the physical relocation of Indian peoples from reservations to urban areas, and hasten the termination, or extinction, of tribes.

Between 1954 and 1962 Congress passed specific laws authorizing the termination of more than 100 tribal groups. The stated purpose of the termination policy was to ensure the full and complete integration of Indians into American society. However, there is a less benign way to interpret this legislation. Even as termination was being discussed in Congress, 133 separate bills were introduced to permit the transfer of trust land ownership from Indians to non-Indians.

With the Johnson administration in the 1960s the federal government began to reject termination. In the 1970s yet another Indian policy emerged. Known as "self-determination," it favored keeping the protective role of the federal government while increasing tribal participation in, and control of, important areas of local government. In 1983 President Reagan, in a policy statement on Indian affairs, restated the unique "government to government" relationship of the United States with the Indians. However, federal programs since then have moved toward transferring Indian affairs to individual states, which have long desired to gain control of Indian land and resources.

As long as American Indians retain power, land, and resources that are coveted by the states and the federal government, there will continue to be a "clash of cultures," and the issues will be contested in the courts, Congress, the White House, and even in the international human rights community. To give all Americans a greater comprehension of the issues and conflicts involving American Indians today is a major goal of this series. These issues are not easily understood, nor can these conflicts be readily resolved. The study of North American Indian history and culture is a necessary and important step toward that comprehension. All Americans must learn the history of the relations between the Indians and the federal government, recognize the unique legal status of the Indians, and understand the heritage and cultures of the Indians of North America.

Narragansett Bay looking out to Dutch Island.

ORIGINS
OF THE
NARRAGANSETT PEOPLE

An early Narragansett legend traces the origin of the tribe's power and influence to a *sachem*, or ruler, whose family was said to be more noble than all others. According to this legend, "In those countries of Narragansett, Niantic, Coweset, and parts adjacent there was one great Sachem who had all the parts under him and ruling over all; his name was Tashtasick. He had only a son and a daughter; and he, esteeming none of degree for them to marry with, married them together." This couple had four sons. Canonicus, the eldest, was sachem in the early 17th century, when the English came to North America.

The tradition that Tashtasick's son and daughter married each other should not be taken literally. The Narragansett had clearly defined principles of kinship and morality that governed their marital behavior. This legend can be seen as a statement that the Narragansett rulers enjoyed greater prestige than other ruling families. Like the pharaohs of ancient Egypt or the royal families of Europe, members of the Narragansett ruling family tended to marry close relatives.

At the time of their greatest authority, the Narragansett had a domain that extended throughout most of what is now Rhode Island from Westerly in the southwest to about Pawtucket and the Blackstone River valley to the northeast and also included Block Island offshore and Conanicut Island in Narragansett Bay. Most of the Narragansett population lived along the shore and in the river valleys and forests on the western side of what is now Narragansett Bay. In the southern New England region around them lived other related groups of people: the Nipmuck and Massachusett to the north, the Pequot and Mohegan to the west, the Sakonnet and Pokanoket, or Wampanoag, to the east across Narragansett Bay. The Narragansett sachems extended their rule over one Massachusett sachemdom, certain Nipmuck bands, the Pokanoket, the eastern Niantic, and a number of small sachemdoms (the Pawtuxet Wampanoag, Coweset, Shawomet, Mashapaug, and Manisseans) near their homeland on Narragansett Bay.

All southern New England Indians, including the Narragansett, spoke related languages of the eastern Algonquian family. People speaking Eastern Algonquian languages lived along the Atlantic coast from as far north as the Maritime Provinces in Canada to as far south as North Carolina. Speakers of one Eastern Algonquian dialect could speak with neighboring groups but had more difficulty being understood by those that lived farther away. The dialects spoken by the Pequot, Mohegan, Massachusett, and Wampanoag were similar to that of the Narragansett and could be understood by them.

The name *Narragansett*, like the names of most tribes in this region, referred to both a place and the people who lived there. Roger Williams, the first English settler of Providence, wrote that the name came from that of a small island, which he did not locate precisely but which may have been in what is now Point Judith Pond. He went to the island but could not learn why the Indians called it Narragansett. Some present-day Narragansett believe that it means "people of the little points and bays." A linguist who has studied the word believes that it means "at the small narrow point of land." Early English writers spelled it in a variety of ways, such as Nanohigganset, Nahigonset, and Nahicans. The present-day

town of Narragansett was part of the domain of the Narragansett ruling family, which was centered in what is now North Kingstown and South Kingstown.

The Narragansett (like all other North American Indian groups) did not have an alphabetic form of writing. They recorded selected events in symbols drawn upon or cut into rock surfaces. Thus there are no detailed written accounts of their past. For information about Indian life in this area prior to the written records of Europeans that begin the historic period, we must turn to the findings of archaeologists. Through excavation of former villages and campsites, a story of a very stable way of life going back many generations and thousands of years is coming to light. The Narragansett live in an area that was home to very ancient populations, and they may well be descended from people who came into the region more than 10,000 years ago. Indeed, their tradition is that their forebears came long, long ago from the north and west into what is now southeastern New England.

In North America as a whole, the archaeological record shows three main periods that preceded the contact period, when Europeans arrived. The earliest is the Paleo-Indian period, when human beings first migrated from Asia to North America, perhaps 15,000 to 20,000 years ago. At that time, the climate was much colder, and parts of North America were covered with glacial ice. What is now the open sea of the Bering Strait was then an expanse of land bridging the two continents, and people as well as animals could easily move across it.

The Paleo-Indians hunted large cold-weather herd animals, such as mammoths, mastodons, and bison, that lived in this Arctic environment. A site that was inhabited by these earliest hunters can be identified from artifacts showing their technology. In particular, they manufactured a distinctive type of stone spear point that had a flute or hollow chipped out of each side. A fluted point could be securely hafted, or fastened to a wooden shaft to form a hunting weapon. Such points have been found at archaeological sites in New England, including the Narragansett Bay area, and date to about 11,000 years ago. The Paleo-Indians who made these spear points were the first people known to have lived in southern New England. Their way of life ended when the climate warmed up, the glaciers melted, and the large cold-weather animals died off. Melting glaciers added water to the oceans, causing the sea level to rise. For this reason, many Paleo-Indian campsites have disappeared beneath the sea.

The people who came after these Paleo-Indians found other ways to make a living. The warming climate made possible a greater diversity of plant and animal species. The next archaeological period, known as the Archaic, lasted from about 10,000 years ago to about 700 B.C. in the Northeast. Archaic people hunted a wider range of smaller

Records deeply incised (carved) into a drilled rock that probably was a hammer stone, found during excavation of a 17th-century Indian cemetery at Burr's Hill, near Sowams, Rhode Island.

forest animals and learned efficient ways to gather other food resources, such as fish, shellfish, seeds, nuts, roots, and berries. Hunters of the Archaic also manufactured a greater variety of stone tools than the Paleo-Indians did. These included tools for cutting and sharpening wood, such as grooved axes, grooved adzes, and gouges. The presence of such tools indicates that these people spent a great deal of effort on woodworking, most

A few of the artifacts found during excavation of a Terminal Archaic cremation burial site at West Ferry on Conanicut Island in Narragansett Bay.

likely to construct houses and dugout canoes.

Later, or Terminal, Archaic Indians, who lived from about 1700 B.C. to 700 B.C., gave special attention to the way they buried their dead. They often cremated the bodies, burying the charcoal and bone ashes together in a large pit that they filled with a wealth of stone and shell implements. Archaeologists have excavated one such Terminal Archaic cremation burial at the West Ferry site on Conanicut Island in Narragansett Bay. There they found burned human bones, much charcoal, numerous spear and arrow points, a stone pestle,

a polished stone adze blade, a polished and grooved stone axhead, a decorated stone pendant, a decorated slate tablet, bowls carved out of steatite (soapstone), a decorated shell, crushed red hematite (iron ore), and black graphite. The stone pestle was surely used to prepare food by pounding seeds, nuts, and roots. The ax and adze were used to cut and plane wood. The steatite bowls varied in size from small individual serving bowls to a large kettle that could have served an entire camp. The people living here had quarried the steatite for bowls and pendants from rock outcrops in what is now the Oaklawn area of Cranston and near the foot of Neutaconcanut Hill in Johnston, Rhode Island. The crushed red hematite and black graphite were paint pigments that probably had symbolic importance in the ritual of cremation and burial. These Terminal Archaic people had more goods and more wealth than their predecessors had, and they buried much of it with their dead.

In the Northeast the time from 700 B.C. to about A.D. 1500 is known as the Woodland period. The economy changed from one based entirely upon hunting and gathering wild foods to one based upon a combination of gardening, hunting, and gathering. The Woodland people learned how to grow corn, beans, and squash to supplement wild foods. They also grew tobacco, which was used during ceremonies, for healing, and as a stimulant. They learned to make pottery, which replaced the earlier soapstone bowls. Numerous sites around Narragansett Bay contain thick deposits of clam and oyster shells, bones of food animals, and brown potsherds (broken pieces of pottery) from the Woodland period. The characteristic arrow point from this time is triangular and is made of white quartz or green shale. Gardening supplemented but did not replace the ancient reliance on wild food; people still ate the deer, fish, shellfish, ducks, nuts, and berries they got by hunting, fishing, and gathering. But the foods they grew made a big difference: Populations increased throughout the Woodland period, probably supported by the greater food supply made possible by growing crops and storing the surpluses. As the size of communities increased and more communities were established, leaders and ruling families became more important.

The Narragansett whom the earliest New England Europeans knew were the direct heirs to the traditions of this long line of prehistoric people who had lived in the Narragansett Bay area for thousands of years. They were a populous group: One early Rhode Island colonist estimated their number to be around 30,000, whereas ethnohistorian Neal Salisbury thinks that a realistic figure would be between 35,000 and 40,000, including the groups controlled by the Narragansett at that time, such as the Shawomet, Pawtuxet, Coweset, and Niantic.

In the 16th and 17th centuries Europeans came to New England looking for land and wealth. Many settled in the region, setting up farms and towns on land that had long been used by the Narragansett and their related Indian subjects and neighbors. The newcomers traded European manufactured goods—glass beads, iron knives, axes, hoes, and brass kettles—to the Indians in return for furs. The Indians eagerly sought to replace their stone and shell tools with the clearly more effective tools made of iron. The Narragansett were excellent traders. Because they were located on the coast, they and the Pequot became intermediaries. They exchanged European goods with more remote tribes for a higher price in furs than they originally paid. By controlling trade routes and determining trading values, the sachems became wealthy and influential.

The Narragansett called the English *Chauquaquock*, or "knife-men." This name suggests that the Narragansett thought of the contrast between European and Indian ways of life in material as well as symbolic terms: They recognized that the English differed from the Narragansett as iron does from stone. ▲

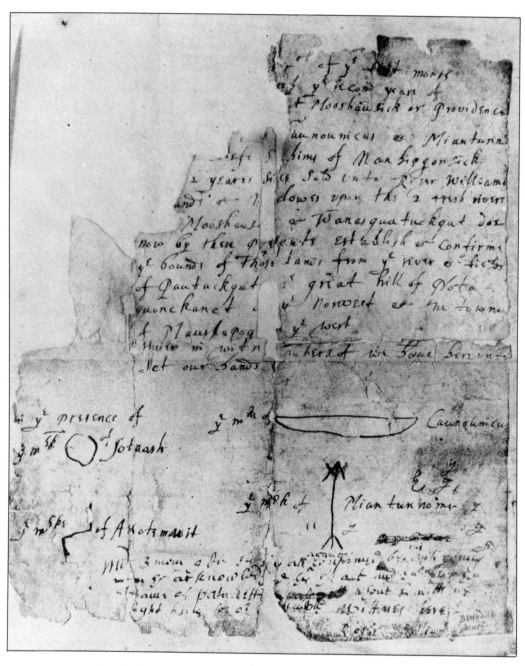

The deed with the signs of the sachems Canonicus (a bow) and Miantonomi (an arrow), giving Roger Williams title to land in Rhode Island.

A WAY OF LIFE
AT THE
THRESHOLD OF HISTORY

The first European known to have visited Narragansett Bay was also the first to write about the Narragansett people. Giovanni da Verrazano, an Italian navigator, observed that they were handsome, friendly, and shy. In the spring of 1524 he wrote:

> These people are the most beautiful and have the most civil customs that we have found on this voyage. They are taller than we are . . . the face is clear-cut . . . the eyes are black and alert, and their manner is sweet and gentle.

Verrazano, a keen observer, remained among them for 15 days. "The animals," he wrote:

> which are in great numbers, as stags, deer, lynxes, and many other species, are taken by snares, and by bows, the latter being their chief implement; their arrows are wrought with great beauty, and for the heads of them,

they use . . . sharp stones, in the place of iron. They also use the same kind of sharp stones in cutting down trees, and with them they construct their boats of single logs, hollowed out with admirable skill, and sufficiently commodious to contain ten or twelve persons.

For almost a century after Verrazano's visit, the Narragansett way of life continued with few interruptions from outsiders. By the early 1600s, however, increased numbers of Dutch, French, and English were venturing into their waters to catch fish and to trade for furs. Although these earliest voyagers did not settle on Narragansett shores, they brought with them diseases that had previously been unknown among the Indians, such as plague, smallpox, and tuberculosis.

Then, in 1620, the English Pilgrims established a permanent settlement on the site of a Pawtuxet Wampanoag village whose population had been deci-

An 1844 engraving shows the first meeting between Roger Williams and the Narragansett as described in a traditional legend.

mated by European disease. Within a decade Englishmen and -women were pouring into settlements around Boston and Massachusetts Bay. In 1636 the first English settlers appeared in Narragansett country. A small band, led by Roger Williams, a Puritan minister, built permanent homes alongside the tidal marshes on the east side of the Providence and Moshassuck rivers. The Puritans, a highly disciplined and strictly moral Protestant sect that followed the teachings of John Calvin and opposed Catholicism, felt that the Old World was corrupt. They had come to the New World, and especially to Massachusetts, in order to create an ideal society in a new land. Williams, however, had questioned some of the ideas of the Puritan leaders. In particular, he had advocated the separation of the church from the governing structure of the

Massachusetts Bay Colony, and he had been expelled by the colony as a religious radical.

According to an old Providence English legend, the Narragansett greeted Williams at Slate Rock on the east bank of the Seekonk River with the words "What cheer, Netop." "What cheer" was an English greeting that they had already learned. "Netop" was the Narragansett word for friend. In welcoming the first English settlers to Providence they took a large step from which there was no turning back.

The English people who colonized the Narragansett country interrupted a successful way of life that had formed over many generations. We know about this way of life from two kinds of sources: archaeology and early historical records. Through excavation of Narragansett camps and villages, archaeologists have learned a great deal about the tools they used, the foods they ate, the ornaments they wore, the homes they built, and how they buried their dead. In the writings of European explorers and settlers who knew them directly are numerous details that support and expand on the archaeological record. Williams, who founded Providence, wrote a book that is the most important account of Narragansett society and culture in the 17th century, *A Key Into the Language of America*. He wrote extensively of their language, religion, family life, hunting, fishing, farming, warfare, and many other topics. Published in London in 1643, Williams's work is one of the earliest and most important books about any native American people.

Both archaeological evidence and early written accounts confirm that the Narragansett lived closely with nature in an environment that was rich in food resources. In spring, when the snow melted and the brooks and rivers rose, they caught many kinds of fish, including alewives, or buckies, that migrated from the sea to freshwater rivers to deposit their eggs. In May they prepared fields along the shores of Narragansett Bay, where women would plant corn, beans, squash, and other edible plants. Men helped the women with the heavy work of clearing new fields, but women did most of the other tasks, such as hoeing, planting, weeding, and harvesting. Men grew their own tobacco, which they smoked in pipes made of stone or clay. Families put up bark-cov-

ered houses, or *wigwams*, near these fields, where women and girls tended the gardens, picked strawberries and other wild fruits, and gathered clams, quahogs, oysters, and lobsters. Each family built watchhouses by its fields, where family members would sometimes even sleep in order to protect the crops from the many hungry birds that would fly in for an early morning meal.

In late summer and fall, the women harvested their crops. They dried the corn in the sun by day and covered it with mats to keep it dry at night. They stored surplus dried corn and beans in baskets, which they put aside and sometimes even buried for later use.

Fragments of basketry and of bark matting (top) such as that used by the Indians of the Northeast to cover their homes.

According to William Harris, an early English settler of Providence, they were able to grow much more corn when they began using English trade axes and hoes with iron blades in place of the stone, shell, and wooden implements they made themselves. Williams and Harris both reported that the woman of a family could raise as many as 60 bushels of corn each year. In fall and winter, families hiked to the interior forests, where they hunted deer, rabbits, squirrels, bears, wildcats, beavers, and other animals for meat and fur. As winter approached, groups of related families left the coastal farming sites and moved to sheltered wooded inland valleys, where they set up cozy winter villages. Here they continued to get meat by hunting and ice fishing. They also ate dried corn, beans, chestnuts, and other foods they had stored. Their winter houses resembled the summer wigwams except that they were roofed with mats rather than with bark for added insulation. In spring they dismantled their winter villages and moved to fishing sites to begin the cycle again.

Roger Williams described the size of Narragansett houses in relation to the number of family members living in them and noted the cooperation that characterized daily life. "Two Families," he wrote, "will live comfortably and lovingly in a little round house of

Blank for making pipe bowl, iron file, and pipe bowl. Iron was one of the most important items the Indians obtained in trade with Europeans. With iron tools the Narragansett could shape stone, shell, and wooden utensils more quickly than with tools made from stone.

some fourteen or sixteen foot over, and so more and more families in proportion." The cooperation, Williams observed, extended to all manner of work: "When a field is to be broken up, they have a very loving sociable speedy way to dispatch it: All the neighbours men and Women forty, fifty, a hundred etc., joyne, and come in to help freely. With friendly joyning they breake up their fields, build their Forts, hunt the Woods, stop and kill fish in the Rivers."

Williams admired their generosity toward one another and toward the English, a generosity that was expressed with both food and land. They understood that survival in times of scarcity could depend on being sure of the generosity of neighbors, and they gave to others what they expected they could receive themselves if they were in need. Given their emphasis on cooperation and generosity, they seldom turned to crime to satisfy their needs. Williams wrote that robbers and murderers were less common among the Narragansett and other Indian groups than among the English and French.

At the time of their first contact with Europeans, the Narragansett believed that an important god, Cautantowwit, had created human beings, and that the souls of dead people returned to his house in the southwest. According to their creation account, Cautantowwit had first made the original man and woman from a stone. Dissatisfied with his work, he broke them in pieces and made a second man and woman from a tree. This second couple became the ancestors of all humanity. In their religious gatherings, known in their language as a *nickommo* (translated by Williams as "feast" or "dance"), the Narragansett dedicated many of their prized possessions to their creator by either giving them to others as gifts or burning them in a fire. They held the nickommo regularly at harvesttime and in midwinter as well as during special emergencies such as drought, famine, sickness, and war. They also buried valuable implements (mats, pots, spoons, knives, tobacco pipes, and axes) and ornaments (beads, ear pendants, and amulets) with the body of a dead person. They may have believed that such objects had souls that would accompany the soul of the dead person to Cautantowwit's afterworld. A wise elder had the responsibility of burying the dead. He would place the body in a shallow oval pit, with knees drawn up to the chest and the head pointed toward the southwest, the direction of the afterworld. No one would mention the name of a person who had recently died. Anyone who had the same name as the deceased would take another name. To speak the name of a recently dead person would have been offensive to the bereaved relatives, who might even attack the offender for showing disrespect. Those who were in mourning for a deceased relative would blacken their faces with soot for weeks. In the case of the death of a tribal leader, his or her followers blackened their faces for a year. When mourning was long past, the name of the deceased

(continued on page 26)

NARRAGANSETT COOKERY

The Narragansett had an ample, varied, and nutritious diet, thanks to the farming done by the women and the abundant natural food sources available to them. The women prepared many interesting dishes by combining their staple crops with the seafood and wild plant foods they collected and the game the men hunted. They cooked a kind of stew from venison (deer meat) and corn in clay pots over the family fire. They stewed or grilled wild ducks, pigeons, fish, and shellfish. Several kinds of berries and nuts, various herbs, wild onions, and fruits added taste, texture, and variety to their meals.

The women ground corn in a mortar, crushing the kernels to make a fine cornmeal. They mixed this with crushed wild strawberries to form a dough, which they baked over an open fire to make a tasty kind of bread. The women also boiled clams to make a briny broth that they used instead of salt to give flavor to their cornmeal bread. Here are two recipes, adapted from a modern Narragansett cookbook, that still show influences of the Narragansett cooking described by Roger Williams some three and a half centuries ago. Both of these recipes call for johnnycake meal. This fine white cornmeal, which many Narragansetts and other New Englanders still eat today, is a distinctive Rhode Island product, available from such companies as the Kenyon Corn Meal Company of Usquepangh. (In these recipes, the more widely available, coarser variety of stone-ground cornmeal is not an adequate substitute.) Johnnycakes are, in fact, a particular type of pancake that is a

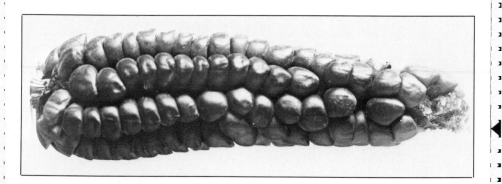

Rhode Island specialty. The name johnnycake is probably derived from the Narragansett word *nokehick*, which meant parched cornmeal. Roger Williams wrote in 1643 that while traveling with Narragansett hunters and warriors, "With a *spoonfull* of this *meale* and a *spoonfull* of water from the *Brooke*, have I made many a good dinner and supper."

JOHNNYCAKE WITH BERRIES

2 cups johnnycake white stone-ground cornmeal	1 cup blueberries or sliced strawberries
1/4 teaspoon salt	1/4 cup cream or milk
2 cups boiling water	corn oil or sunflower oil
4 tablespoons maple syrup	

Combine cornmeal and salt in a bowl. Stir in boiling water and mix until smooth. Add maple syrup and berries and stir thoroughly to combine. Mixture should be somewhat stiff. If it is too stiff, thin with cream or milk. Add a few tablespoons of oil to griddle or skillet, preferably cast iron, and heat until a drop of water just sizzles. Drop batter by tablespoon onto griddle and cook for 5 minutes without turning. Turn and cook for 5 minutes on the other side. Serve plain or with additional maple syrup. Makes 4 to 6 servings.

CORNMEAL PORRIDGE

1 cup johnnycake white stone-ground cornmeal	3 cups shellfish liquid (or bottled clam juice)
1 cup cold water	

Place cornmeal in sturdy saucepan. Stir in water and mix thoroughly. Place over medium heat and add shellfish liquid gradually, 1 cup at a time, stirring constantly. When mixture comes to a bubbling boil, reduce heat and simmer for 10 minutes or longer, stirring frequently, until thick and smooth. This can be served instead of rice or potatoes with fish or seafood dishes. It can be eaten immediately or poured into a pan, allowed to cool, cut into individual portions, and fried. Serves 4 to 6.

Source: Ella Thomas Sekatau, *Narragansett Indian Recipes.* Charlestown, RI: 1973.

(continued from page 23)

could come back into use. For example, the sachem Canonicus died in 1647. By the 1670s the sachem Pessacus had changed his name to Canonicus.

Roger Williams wrote that the great god Cautantowwit had given the people the seeds of the first corn and beans. In Narragansett mythology, the crow brought from Cautantowwit's field the first grain of corn in one ear and the first bean in the other. For this reason the Narragansett generally did not kill crows, even though these birds raided their gardens.

Rarely does a religion depend upon only one supernatural figure. Christians, for example, speak of God the Father, Jesus his son, the Holy Spirit, the Virgin Mary, angels, the devil, saints, and ghosts. So, too, the Narragansett believed in a large number of deities, each of which had control over certain aspects of human life and the natural order. A spirit known as Chepi was second in importance to the creator Cautantowwit. Chepi resembled the European and American notion of a ghost. The Narragansett believed that Chepi was descended from the souls of dead people, and they feared that the spirit would appear in cold, dark, windy places.

The Narragansett and their other southern New England neighbors, such as the Pequot, Mohegan, Wampanoag, and Massachusett, feared Chepi, for they believed that this spirit would punish them when they behaved improperly. For example, early in the colonial period a group of Indians living among the English in Boston saw an alarming vision of Chepi, who warned them against becoming like the English and giving up their Indian ways. In this respect, Chepi acted as an overseer of the traditional way of life. Chepi's role was not completely negative, however, for he played an important part in Narragansett medicine. Tribal healers, known in the Narragansett language as *pawwaws*, gained their power to heal through the help of the spirit Chepi. (The Narragansett word *pawwaw* is the source of the modern word "powwow," used to describe American Indian gatherings anywhere in North America as well as to refer to any type of meeting or discussion.) To this spirit they attributed the power to make rain, drive away evil spirits that caused illness, and even to cause illness among the pawwaw's enemies.

To the early historic-period Narragansett and their neighbors, spirits, or *manitto*, lived everywhere. Specific manitto controlled the sun, moon, sea, and fire. Others presided over the directions (such as the southwest and northeast), colors, houses, men, women, and children. Dreams were important, for spirits spoke to individuals through dreams. In his account of Narragansett culture, Roger Williams commented on the importance of the supernatural: "There is a generall Custome amongst them, at the apprehension of any Excellency in Men, Women, Birds, Beasts, Fish, etc. to cry out *Manittoo*, that is, it is a God, as thus if they see one man excell others in Wisdome,

Valour, strength, Activity etc. they cry out *Manittoo A God.*" Because of their belief in the godliness of unusual or outstanding phenomena, they first perceived Europeans to be gods. Williams wrote, "When they talke amongst themselves of the *English* ships, and great buildings, of the plowing of their Fields, and especially of Bookes and Letters, they will end thus: *Manittowock* They are Gods."

Thus the Narragansett and their Indian neighbors at first thought of Europeans in supernatural and mythical terms. The Indians around Massachusetts Bay, immediately to the north of Narragansett country, thought that the first European ship they saw was a floating island with some trees growing upon it that had broken free of the mainland. The Pokanoket Wampanoag people in the vicinity of what is now Dighton, Massachusetts, told stories of a giant bird that flew into their country carrying white people. This bird reportedly tried to take Indian hostages, but they fought back and prevented it from doing so. According to a legend of the Narragansett, they had heard the sound of a particular hymn in the air several years before the Pilgrims settled at Plymouth. Later, when the Narragansett visited the Pilgrim church, they heard the people there singing the very same hymn that they had heard in the air many years before. As a result, after the Narragansett converted to Christianity in the 18th century, they included this hymn in their religious services.

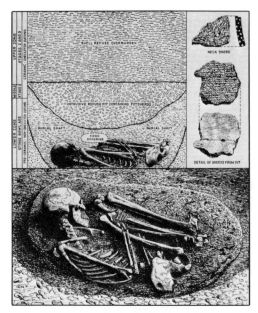

Excavations at burial sites reveal that the Narragansett buried treasured objects, such as tools, pottery, and ornaments, as well as food, with their dead. The body was positioned with knees bent up to the chest and the head toward the southwest, where the Indians believed the afterworld was located.

English technology, and especially the uses of metal, also seemed miraculous to them. Not only could Indian women raise more corn with iron hoes than they could with hoes made of stone, wood, or shell, but the men could clear larger fields with steel axes, kill game at a greater distance with European firearms, and drill more shell beads (*wampum*) with steel drills. The English practice of writing things down on paper also seemed miraculous to the Indians. The Narragansett and other Indians did not have a way of writing their language. They passed knowledge

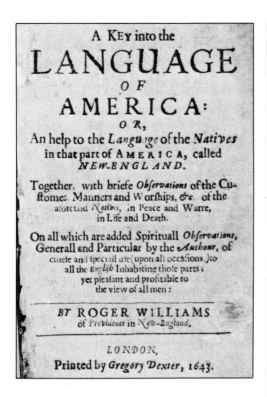

A *Qunnihticut* [Connecticut] Indian (who had heard our discourse) told the *Sachim Miantunnomu*, that soules went up to Heaven, or downe to Hell; For, saith he, Our Fathers have told us, that our soules goe to the *Southwest*.

The *Sachim* answered, But how doe you know your selfe, that your soules goe to the *Southwest*; did you ever see a soule goe thither?

The Native replyed; when did he (naming my selfe) [that is, naming Roger Williams] see a soule goe to Heaven or Hell?

The *Sachim* againe replied: He hath books and writings, and one which God himselfe made, concerning mens soules, and therefore may well know more than wee that have none, but take all upon trust from our forefathers.

The title page of Roger Williams's book explaining Narragansett words and customs.

and memories of past events from one generation to the next by word of mouth. In *A Key Into the Language of America*, Roger Williams reported a conversation between a Narragansett sachem and a Connecticut Indian that indicates the greater authority the Narragansett attributed to the English written word over the Indian spoken word. It also shows that even before 1643, when Williams wrote this account, the Narragansett sachem Miantonomi (Miantunnomu) had already begun to question Indian religious belief in light of what he knew about the Bible.

The sachem was arguing that English writing was more accurate than Indian oral tradition and that, therefore, English religious beliefs as recorded in the Bible might also be more true than their Indian counterparts.

Another Indian deity, known as Wetucks or Maushop, was a very industrious giant who helped the Indians and taught them how to make a living. This giant waded into the sea to catch whales, which he ate but also shared with the Indians. According to legends that survived among the Wampanoag neighbors of the Narragansett, this giant rolled boulders into the sea so that he could wade farther away from shore to pursue whales. The Wampanoag of

THE HYMN HEARD IN THE AIR

The Narragansett and other Indians in the Northeast heard the music of this hymn in the air years before Europeans arrived among them. They heard the music again when they first visited the Pilgrims' church at Plymouth. The hymn is sung to this day, with the following words whose author is unknown.

Glory to God the Father be, Glory to God the Son,
Glory to God the Holy Ghost, Glory to God alone.
    Hallelujah, Hallelujah, Hosanna, Hosanna,
    Hallelujah, Hallelujah, Hosanna, Hosanna.

My soul doth magnify the Lord, My spirit doth rejoice
In God my Saviour, and my God: I hear a joyful voice.
    Hallelujah, Hallelujah, Hosanna, Hosanna,
    Hallelujah, Hallelujah, Hosanna, Hosanna.

I need not go abroad for joy, I have a feast at home;
My sighs are turned into songs, The Comforter is come.
    Hallelujah, Hallelujah, Hosanna, Hosanna,
    Hallelujah, Hallelujah, Hosanna, Hosanna.

Down from above the blessed Dove, Is come into my breast,
To witness God's eternal love, This is my heavenly feast.
    Hallelujah, Hallelujah, Hosanna, Hosanna,
    Hallelujah, Hallelujah, Hosanna, Hosanna.

This makes me Abba, Father, cry, With confidence of soul;
It makes me cry, My Lord, my God, and that without control.
    Hallelujah, Hallelujah, Hosanna, Hosanna,
    Hallelujah, Hallelujah, Hosanna, Hosanna.

There is a stream that issues forth from God's eternal throne,
And from the Lamb, a living stream, Clear as a crystal stone.
    Hallelujah, Hallelujah, Hosanna, Hosanna,
    Hallelujah, Hallelujah, Hosanna, Hosanna.

Source: Thomas Commuck,
Indian Melodies. New York:
G. Lane and C.B. Tippett, 1845.

Scene in a New England Indian village, drawn from accounts by modern Narragansett and research by anthropologists, archaeologists, geologists, and other authorities.

Gay Head on Martha's Vineyard still tell today about how Maushop built a rock formation known as the Devil's Bridge in the shallow water off the Gay Head peninsula. One legend tells how he became angry when the English crowded into his territory, and in his anger he threw his wife from Gay Head to Sakonnet Point in Little Compton on the eastern mouth of Narragansett Bay. There she can be seen today as Sakonnet Rock, in the water off Sakonnet Point. The Wampanoag people of Gay Head also still refer to fog as smoke from Maushop's pipe. Another Wampanoag legend tells how Maushop created Nantucket Island by emptying the ashes from his giant pipe into the sea. Nantucket, they say, is the Devil's Ash Heap. Such legends are reminders of a time when the Narragansett and other New England Indians saw their entire world and landscape as alive with supernatural activities. In their legends, the rocks, land formations, and waterways had many meanings.

Just as the Narragansett organized their religious world into a ranked series of greater and lesser gods, each with different responsibilities, they organized their society into a hierarchy of greater and lesser chiefs and healers. The sachems came from royal families, in which power was inherited, usually by a son from his father. Most sachems were men, but there were a few women who held this position. Some women became sachem when their brothers or husbands died or when there was no brother or other man in the family to inherit the title from a father. Some sachems ruled over small localities that consisted of only one village. Other sachems had vast domains. The sachem Canonicus was ruling over all local sachems when the English first settled in Rhode Island.

The Narragansett had a pattern of rule by two sachems, on which Verrazano had commented. Canonicus, for example, shared power with his brother's son, the sachem Miantonomi. Canonicus was the senior sachem and his nephew the junior sachem. The junior sachem acted as a kind of ambassador, representing Canonicus when he traveled to meet with other tribes and with the English. Sachems allocated land to those under their authority and collected tribute, such as corn, deerskins, and wild game, from their subjects. They, with their counselors, decided when to go to war, determined the terms of peace agreements, and settled disputes among their followers. The counselors were elders, noted warriors, and members of the sachems' family. The sachems were not authoritarian rulers nor did they have ironclad authority over their dependents. They ruled by consensus, not by voting and determining a majority opinion. Before taking a course of action, they debated the various options until all their counselors were in agreement. If a sachem treated his people cruelly or unfairly, they were free to move to the territory of a sachem who would treat them better. Because having a large number of subjects reflected well on a sachem, tribal leaders were careful to treat their subjects well.

The healers, or pawwaws, were spiritual advisers to the sachems but were under their authority. They could predict the outcome of a battle or other future event, and their predictions were important to the debates of the sachems and council. The pawwaws specialized in performing the Narragansett's yearly rituals at harvesttime and midwinter and in caring for the sick. Unlike the position of sachem, that of pawwaw was not usually hereditary. Pawwaws earned their position through their ability to communicate with the spirit Chepi and by their ability to heal or injure others through sorcery. They could take an object, such as the hair of a person, and turn it into a magical arrow to send back against that person, or they could enchant an actual arrowhead and invoke supernatural powers to make it injure a particular individual. If a pawwaw failed to diagnose an illness correctly or to cure it, the sick patient or that person's relatives might accuse the pawwaw of being a weak healer and go to another for help. Most pawwaws were men. Many women, however, knew the art of making medicine from plants and knew other techniques, such as massaging, that could help the sick. When a woman was ready to give birth, knowledgeable Indian women helped, a practice that lasted into the late 19th century.

The Narragansett respected their elders and cared for the old people in their communities. Family members who lived together probably included three generations—grandparents, parents, and children. There is some evidence that after marriage a woman moved to the residence of her husband's family. Prominent men, such as sachems, often had more than one wife. Because women were responsible for doing much important work, such as planting and tending crops, additional wives contributed to a sachem's wealth. A Narragansett man kept away from his wife from the time her pregnancy became known until after the baby was born and it became old enough not to feed at the mother's breast. This long period of separation between husband and wife, which could be about two or

A wooden bowl for cornmeal porridge. Narragansett men were superb wood-carvers and traded their work to European colonists as well as to other Indians.

three years, is another reason why Narragansett men married more than one woman. The several wives had separate houses, side by side.

English observers exclaimed at how kind, loving, and permissive Indian parents were to their children. Parents taught their children the arts and skills that were necessary for making a living. Men hunted, did the heavy work of clearing patches of forest for fields, grew tobacco, and made stone tools (arrow points and knives) and wooden items (dugout canoes, bows, war clubs, and porridge bowls). They also waged war and engaged in trade. Narragansett men enjoyed a wide reputation among neighboring Indian groups as well as among the English for their industry in trade and their skilled handiwork—making tobacco pipes from steatite and the delicate clamshell bead currency called wampum.

Women did most of the gardening. They carried burdens, gathered shellfish and wild plant foods, such as strawberries and chestnuts, did the heavy work of pulverizing dried corn with stone or wooden pestles in wooden mortars, and were responsible for all other food preparation and cooking. They cared for young children, made baskets, earthen pots, and leather clothing, and set up and took down the wigwams when the family moved.

The best-known female Narragansett sachem in the early historic period was Matantuck, also known as Magnus or Quiapen. Called the Old Queen by the English, this Sunck Squaw, or fe-

Steatite (soapstone) pipe bowl with sculpture of bear and a stone blank ready to be carved into a pipe bowl, both excavated at Burr's Hill. Narragansett men were skilled stone carvers. Indians smoked tobacco during ceremonies and on other ritual occasions.

male sachem, lived until 1676. English and Indian soldiers from Connecticut colony killed her while she was hiding in a swamp in what is now Smithfield, Rhode Island, near the end of King Philip's War. The Queen's Fort, a large structure made of boulders in North Kingstown, Rhode Island, is named for the Old Queen Matantuck. The fort's stone walls were built by Narragansett men from glacial rocks in the area. They are among the most permanent visible reminders of the Narragansett way of life from the period before 1675, when war erupted between the New England Indians and the colonists. ▲

The Roger Williams Memorial Statue is on a bluff overlooking modern Providence, the city that he founded.

COLONIZATION
AND
WAR

The territory on which the Pilgrims landed in 1620 belonged to the Pokanoket Wampanoag sachem Ousamequin, better known as Massasoit. In a sense this territory also belonged to the Narragansett, for they ruled over Massasoit and his people. For some years before the arrival of the Pilgrims, the Narragansett and the Wampanoag had been feuding with each other in competition for trading rights in the Narragansett Bay area, and ultimately the Narragansett had prevailed.

To make Massasoit's situation even worse, European epidemic diseases killed large numbers of his followers from 1616 to 1618. From his point of view, the Pilgrims were potential allies against his former enemies and present overlords. He saw an opportunity to regain independence from the Narragansett sachems by allying the Wampanoag with the English.

The Narragansett resented the new advantage Massasoit achieved through this alliance. In the fall of 1621 they sent a war party out to capture him and his bodyguards. At Plymouth, the English supported their ally, demanding that the Narragansett release him. Canonicus, the Narragansett chief sachem, did not wish to go to war with the English, and so he ordered that Massasoit be released.

Then, in January 1622, a strange episode took place: A bundle of arrows tied together in a snakeskin arrived at Plymouth. Was this a declaration of war from the Narragansett? The English believed that it was—the messenger who brought it identified himself as Narragansett, and the interpreters told them it was a challenge. The English sent the snakeskin, filled with powder and shot, back to Canonicus by another messenger. In this way they let him know that they accepted his challenge. But Canonicus, who feared English witchcraft as well as weapons, refused to accept the snakeskin and had it returned to Plymouth. For the time being, war had been averted.

The feud between the Narragansett and the Wampanoag broke out again the following year. The Narragansett crossed the bay and attacked Massasoit's village at Sowams, now Warren, Rhode Island. Massasoit fled, but his English allies, under Captain Miles Standish, marched to Sowams to meet the Narragansett war party. Canonicus himself arrived with Narragansett reinforcements but suddenly withdrew his men, moving them back to Narragansett country on the east side of the bay.

The Pequot, taking advantage of the Narragansett's military involvement to the east, decided to attack their trading rivals from the west. While the Narragansett warriors massed near the bay to attack Sowams, the Pequot invaded Narragansett lands near what is now Westerly, Rhode Island. Canonicus hastened to defend his western frontier against the Pequot invaders and drove them out of the disputed territory. Once more he avoided a battle with the English, and there were no significant hostile encounters from this time until the 1630s.

For many years, both the Pequot and the Narragansett had been enjoying a prosperous trade with the Dutch,

View from the Treaty Rock, above the Pettaquamscutt River. It is believed that this is where Roger Williams completed the purchase of Providence from the Narragansett.

who did not settle in their territory but who visited by boat. Dutch Island in Narragansett Bay, for example, is most likely named for traders from the Netherlands who had landed there and used it as a trading base. They traded merchandise of European manufacture, such as glass beads and bottles, iron knives, hoes, and hatchets, copper kettles, and white clay pipes, which were being made in Europe as early as the 1620s, for Indian furs. But as English population and power increased in the 1630s, Dutch influence among the Pequot and Narragansett declined.

The Pequot had themselves recently been weakened by a serious epidemic, and they looked to the English of the Massachusetts Bay Colony as allies in their political and economic rivalry with the Narragansett. They had encouraged the English to settle in their homeland along the lower reaches of the Connecticut River in what is now Connecticut. By 1635 English families were moving into the Pequot domain. They, however, considered the Pequot to be their subjects, not their patrons. They required the Pequot to pay them tribute and held them responsible for the deaths of two English traders, Captain John Stone and John Oldham. However, Oldham had actually been killed by people from Block Island who were Narragansett subjects.

In 1636 Roger Williams obtained a large tract of land from Canonicus as a gift. Here, between the Pawtuxet and Seekonk rivers and east of Neutaconcanut Hill, he founded the town of Providence. Other English settled on Aquidneck Island in 1638. In 1639 Williams, who had learned some of the Indian language and had traveled among them as a trader, established a trading post at Cocumscussoc, near present-day Wickford, Rhode Island, close to Canonicus's main village. Perhaps the Narragansett decided that it was now strategic to have their own English allies for protection from the English at Plymouth and Massachusetts Bay.

In 1637 the Narragansett found themselves forced to take sides in a major conflict between two of their long-standing adversaries, the Pequot and the English Puritans of Connecticut and Massachusetts Bay. The year before, an English delegation from Boston had visited the court of Canonicus to persuade him not to side with the Pequot if the English decided to go to war against them. Edward Johnson, a Puritan historian who may have accompanied this delegation, gave a remarkable account of Canonicus's court in *Wonder-Working Providence*, a book published in London in 1654.

The Indian King [Canonicus] hearing of their coming, gathered together his chief Counsellors, and a great number of his Subjects to give them entertainment, resolving as then that the young King [Miantonomi] should receive their message, yet in his hearing. They arriving, were [entertained] royally, with respect to the Indian manner. [Boiled] Chestnuts is their White-bread, which are very sweet, as if they were mixt with

Sugar; and because they would be extraordinary in their feasting, they strive for variety after the English manner, boyling Puddings made of beaten corne, putting therein great store of black berries, somewhat like Currants. They having thus nobly feasted them, afterward give them Audience, in a State-house, round, about fifty foot wide, made of long poles stuck in the ground, like your Summer-houses in England, and covered round about, and on the top with Mats, save a small place in the middle of the Roofe, to give light, and let out the smoke.

In this place sat their Sachim, with very great attendance; the English coming to deliver their Message, to manifest the greater state, the Indian Sachim lay along upon the ground, on a Mat, and his Nobility sat on the ground, with their legs doubled up, their knees touching their chin; with much sober gravity they attend the Interpreters speech. It was matter of much wonderment to the English, to see how solidly and wisely these savage people did consider of the weighty undertaking of a War; especially old Canonicus, who was very discreet in his ansers. . . . [Miantonomi] did willingly embrace peace with the English, considering right well, that although their number was but small in comparison of his people, and that they were but strangers to the Woods, Swamps, and advantagious places of this Wildernesse, yet withall he knew the English were advantaged by their weapons of War, and especially their Guns, which were of

great terror to his people, and also he had heard they came of a more populous Nation by far than all the Indians were, could they be [joined] together. Also on the other hand, with mature deliberation, he was well advised of the Peaquods cruell disposition and aptnesse to make War, as also their neere neighbourhood to his people. . . . Hereupon he demes it most conducing to his owne and his peoples safety to direct his course in a middle way, holding amity with both. The English return home, having gained the old Kings favour so far.

The Pequot also attempted to win the support of the Narragansett and sent ambassadors to them, but Governor John Winthrop of Massachusetts Bay and Roger Williams succeeded in persuading the Narragansett to side with the English. This alliance naturally included the Niantic, who still relied on the Narragansett sachems for protection of their western frontier against the Pequot. The English also gained the support of the Mohegan, under their sachem Uncas. A small sachemdom, the Mohegan had revolted against their Pequot overlords and saw the colonists as protectors for the future.

Hostilities escalated in the spring of 1637. Indians allied with the English killed a Pequot and took his scalp. A party of Pequot warriors attacked an English settlement at Wethersfield on the Connecticut River. In May English forces, along with their Narragansett, Niantic, and Mohegan allies, attacked

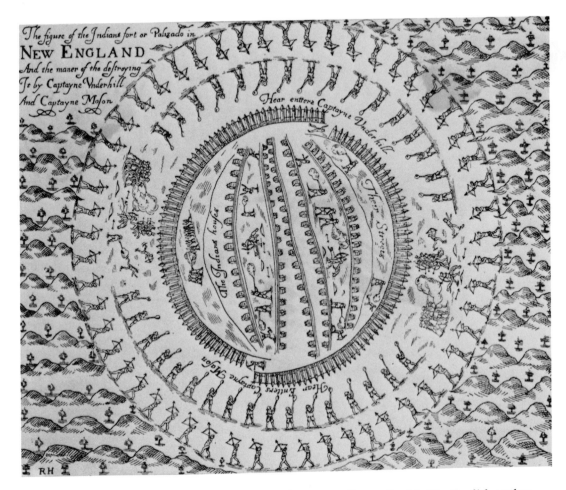

Attack on the Pequot fort (center, shown with the surrounding palisade). The English settlers from Massachusetts Bay and Rhode Island (shown holding muskets) and their Narragansett and other Indian allies (in the outer circle, with bows and arrows) broke through the palisade in two places and easily felled the defenders.

and burned a fortified Pequot village on a hilltop near the Mystic River in southeastern Connecticut.

Having won the battle, the English rounded up and executed many of the Pequot men, dividing the remaining men, women, and children among themselves and their Indian allies as slaves. Thus the English, with Indian help, eliminated the Pequot as an obstacle to the colonization of Connecticut. The Narragansett and Mohegan, by joining forces with the English against the Pequot, gave up forever the possibility of unified Indian resistance to white control.

The Narragansett would soon learn that they had stepped into a trap, for the English turned against them the tactic of pitting Indian against Indian. Although the Narragansett and Mohegan had both supported the English against the Pequot, they did not support each other. The Mohegan were too small a sachemdom to pose a significant threat to the English, whereas the Narragansett were very numerous. When the Narragansett and the Mohegan feuded, the English favored the weaker Mohegan against the stronger Narragansett. By favoring the Mohegan and other nearby Indian groups against the Narragansett, the English were able to undermine Narragansett power to their own advantage. This was to the advantage of Uncas, the Mohegan sachem, as well.

The English also whittled away at the Narragansett domain. Soon, for ex-ample, the governor of the Massachusetts Bay Colony formally assumed control of a Narragansett dependency, the Manissean sachemdom on Block Island. Meanwhile, the Niantic sachem, Janemo, or Ninigret, became increasingly independent from Canonicus and Miantonomi. The English tactic of divide and conquer was successfully separating the Narragansett from the smaller groups over which they had previously exercised control.

Because the English of Providence and Aquidneck Island were independent from those of the Massachusetts Bay and Connecticut colonies, the Narragansett trusted them more. In 1637 and 1638, the Narragansett had willingly deeded the Providence settlers more land from their declining territory. In 1642 Samuel Gorton, whose dissenting religious views had made him unpopular with the Massachusetts

Marks made by the sachem Miantonomi when signing documents.

authorities, along with 11 followers, also obtained land from the Narragansett, including much of what is now Warwick, West Warwick, and Coventry. The settlers named this tract Shawomet.

A few years later, the Massachusetts Bay Colony offended the Narragansett by claiming these same Shawomet lands and other lands bordering on the Pawtuxet River for itself. Two lesser sachems, Pomham of the Shawomet, who lived near Warwick Cove, and Socononoco, sachem of the Pawtuxet, who lived near the mouth of the Pawtuxet River, asserted their independence from Miantonomi, who had taken over many leadership duties from the aging Canonicus. They submitted themselves and their territories to the Massachusetts Bay Colony. Miantonomi realized at this point that his English allies in Providence and on Aquidneck Island were too weak to help him or to protect themselves against power plays by the larger colony at Massachusetts Bay.

In 1638 the English of Massachusetts and Connecticut signed the Hartford Treaty with both the Narragansett and Mohegan. In the event of a quarrel between the two Indian tribes, they had to appeal first to the English of these United Colonies of New England, whose decision would be binding—and who therefore had the opportunity to side with whichever tribe it was to their advantage to support. It would not be long before the Narragansett learned how the Hartford Treaty functioned.

Miantonomi's predicament in the early 1640s was summed up by Howard Chapin in his 1936 book, *Sachems of the Narragansetts*.

> Thus in the space of less than 25 years, he had seen the vast empire of his father shorn of the Wampanoag territory, of Shawomet and of Pawtuxet by revolt. He had seen the Massachusetts Indians steadily but without a blow, withdraw from his domination and submit to the English. He had seen the English conquer and annex his island vassal of Mannases or Block Island, and conquer and annex his Pequot rivals on the West. He had lost the whole of eastern Massachusetts and Block Island. He had sold the northern half of the present Rhode Island, and most of the islands in the Bay, and was surrounded on all sides by English or hostile Indians.

Miantonomi now saw clearly that the neighboring English colonies were after his entire domain. He began to seek a way to reverse the tide of colonization that was pushing ever farther into the Narragansett homeland.

One alternative could be the creation of a new form of Indian leadership that would unite the increasingly weak and isolated Indian groups of the southern New England area. Miantonomi seems to have had such a plan in mind as early as the summer of 1642, when he visited the Montauk people of eastern Long Island. There he spoke eloquently of the need for Indian unification and resistance as the only hope for preserving their future as a people. An Englishman who was present at the time wrote down a translation of Miantonomi's oration:

> For so are we all Indians as the English are [all one people], and say brother to one another; so must we be one as they are, otherwise we shall all be gone shortly, for you know our fathers had plenty of deer and skins, our plains were full of deer, as also our woods, and of turkies, and our coves full of fish and fowl. But these English having gotten our land, they with scythes cut down the grass, and with axes fell the trees; their cows and horses eat the grass, and their hogs spoil our clam banks, and we shall all be starved.

Miantonomi's statement gives a clear view of how serious the Narragansett judged the situation to be. We do not know if he intended to wage war against the English or to increase his bargaining strength by creating an intertribal alliance. Both seem possible. But whatever his intent may have been, the Montauk did not go along with it.

Next came one of the darkest moments in Narragansett history. In 1643 the Narragansett and Mohegan became involved in a series of quarrels. Uncas accused Miantonomi of trying to kill him. A Pequot was accused of having shot Uncas with an arrow, and the sachem displayed a wound as proof, claiming that the Pequot was a secret assassin sent by the Narragansett. The Pequot claimed that Uncas had paid him to stage the episode and that the sachem had cut himself with a knife.

The next conflict, however, was indisputable: Miantonomi led a war party of about 1,000 men west into Mohegan country to punish the Mohegan for threatening a small Connecticut tribe that was allied to the Narragansett. An English follower of Samuel Gorton at Shawomet had lent Miantonomi a heavy suit of English armor to protect him in battle. Although the Narragansett outnumbered the Mohegan by about two to one, Uncas was able to gain an advantage by pretending to negotiate and then launching a surprise attack on the unsuspecting Narragansett. The Narragansett retreated. Miantonomi, slowed down by his heavy armor, could not escape and was captured by a Mohegan. The magistrates of the United Colonies of New England sensed their opportunity to eliminate the most effective Narragansett leader, and at the same time to pass the blame on to Uncas. They sent secret orders to the Mohegans, and Uncas's brother killed Miantonomi with a hatchet. Uncas then cut a piece of flesh from Miantonomi's shoulder and ate it in a celebration of victory over his longtime rival. By this act the Mohegan chief symbolically acquired the strength of his enemy.

For many years after Miantonomi's death, Narragansett visitors to the site of his capture and burial near Norwich, Connecticut, would drop a stone as a

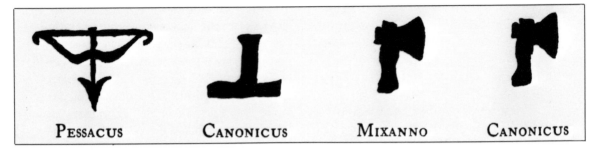

PESSACUS   CANONICUS   MIXANNO   CANONICUS

Marks used by Narragansett sachems to sign treaties in the 17th century.

gesture of mourning and respect to the memory of their sachem. John W. DeForest, whose *History of the Indians of Connecticut* (1853) gives a detailed account of Narragansett-Mohegan warfare, commented on this custom.

> A heap of stones was raised over the grave, and, for a long time afterwards, every Narragansett who passed that way added one or more to the pile. During many subsequent years, parties of this tribe used to visit the spot every September [the anniversary of the death of Miantonomi]. . . . On reaching the rude monument they would break forth into lamentations, and then throwing new stones upon the heap, would consecrate them with mournful cries.

With such monuments, Indian people throughout New England remembered the lives of important people and close relatives. This practice continued in the Wampanoag community of Mashpee, Massachusetts, into the 20th century.

After the death of Miantonomi, Canonicus resumed leadership of the Narragansett, now assisted by the dead sachem's brother, Pessacus. Pessacus promptly sent gifts of wampum to the governor of the Massachusetts Bay Colony and asked for permission to attack Uncas and avenge his brother's death. The governor refused to permit the attack.

Samuel Gorton, who had his own problems with Massachusetts Bay and had recently been imprisoned there, gave the Narragansett sachems a new idea. He suggested that they could protect themselves from New England Puritan aggression by submitting themselves and their domain directly to King Charles of England. True, such an act meant that they would no longer be an independent people. However, if they declared their loyalty to King Charles, their English colonial neighbors would then be obliged to treat them with the political and legal respect due all English subjects. The Narragansett liked this idea. In 1644 the sachems Pessacus and Mixanno (the son and eventual heir of Canonicus) presented their submission in writing to Gorton and three other Englishmen to be carried to the king.

Their letter of allegiance would be of little use to the Narragansett for another 20 years. Unfortunately for them, King Charles was losing power in England. In 1645 Oliver Cromwell and his Puritan army defeated Charles's forces at the Battle of Naseby. That same year the Puritan colonies of New England declared war on the Narragansett. They did so to punish the Indians for their independent course and to eliminate the possibility of a future Narragansett war against them. To avoid being attacked by Plymouth, Massachusetts Bay, and Connecticut, the sachems Pessacus and Mixanno agreed to pay the English 2,000 fathoms of white wampum, the Indian shell currency that had become the medium of trade for the English as well as the Indians, and to give up any claim to the Pequot country. (Six white wampum beads, or two black, were worth one English penny. Twelve pennies, or 72 beads, equalled a shilling. A fathom consisted of 360 white wampum beads and had a value of 5 shillings. The Narragansett sold their land for 720,000 white beads, or £500.)

The power of the Narragansett continued to decline. More and more they found themselves living like tenants on their own land, subject to eviction if they could not meet the payments. In 1646 a delegation of Narragansett and

Niantic went to Boston because they had not made their wampum payment on time. They tried to negotiate a compromise with the commissioners to get an extension of time in which to make the payment. In 1650 they again fell behind in their payments. This time, an armed English force marched to their country to collect, but Roger Williams prevented bloodshed by stepping in front of the angry English captain who was threatening the sachem Pessacus with a pistol.

In 1660 Narragansett war parties attacked the Mohegan in retaliation for various reasons, including their long-standing grievance against the Mohegan for having executed Miantonomi. The Narragansett troops also shot bullets into an English house and frightened an Englishwoman who witnessed one of the attacks. The United Colonies demanded that they pay a fine of 595 fathoms of wampum (214,200 white beads, or about £150) and sent a military force to collect it. Unable to pay the fine, the Narragansett and Niantic sachems mortgaged their lands to the United Colonies. If the Indians failed to make payments, they would lose their lands to the mortgage-holding colonial government. As a short-term solution, the Narragansett made an arrangement with Major Humphrey Atherton and other land speculators who formed a company for this purpose. The English speculators would pay the fine for them, with the understanding that if they could not repay Atherton, he and his associates would take possession of

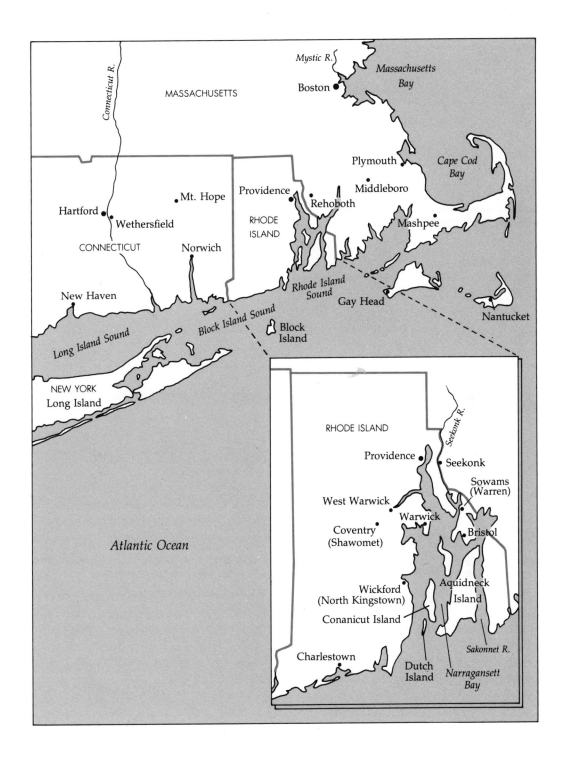

Connecticut R.

MASSACHUSETTS

Mystic R.

Massachusetts Bay

Boston

Plymouth

Cape Cod Bay

Mt. Hope

Providence

Middleboro

Hartford

Wethersfield

RHODE ISLAND

Rehoboth

Mashpee

CONNECTICUT

Norwich

New Haven

Rhode Island Sound

Gay Head

Block Island Sound

Block Island

Nantucket

Long Island Sound

NEW YORK
Long Island

Atlantic Ocean

RHODE ISLAND

Seekonk R.

Providence

Seekonk

Sowams (Warren)

West Warwick

Warwick

Bristol

Coventry (Shawomet)

Wickford (North Kingstown)

Aquidneck Island

Conanicut Island

Charlestown

Sakonnet R.

Dutch Island

Narragansett Bay

Treaty Rock, where Roger Williams bought Providence from the Narragansett, was also where the Atherton Company foreclosed the Indians' mortgage on their lands in 1662.

the Indians' land. Although there is evidence that the Narragansett succeeded in raising the necessary amount of wampum before the deadline set by the speculators, the Atherton Company refused to accept payment. In 1662 the Narragansett sachem Scuttop, son of sachem Mixanno and the Old Queen, formally transferred the land to the English. The speculators now claimed legal title to what remained of the Narragansett's territory—some 400 square miles in southern Rhode Island. In 1664 Scuttop and his sister Quinimiquet declared themselves subjects of the United Colonies.

However, the Rhode Island colony refused to recognize the Atherton group's claim and the Narragansett submission. Rhode Island saw it as an illegal trick by Connecticut and Massachusetts people to acquire land in their colony. The new English king, Charles II, agreed. In 1665 his commissioners in New England confirmed that the Narragansett had long ago offered their submission to Charles I and that their sachemdom belonged to the crown. The king's representatives claimed the Narragansett country in his name as the King's Province and put it under the authority of the Rhode Island colony. The Narragansett were thus protected for the time being from domination by Massachusetts, Plymouth, and Connecticut.

But events to the east of Narragansett Bay, in the area of Plymouth colony and the homeland of the Wampanoag, were soon to have a deadly impact on the Narragansett. The Wampanoag sachem Massasoit was followed at his death by his son Wamsutta, or Alexander; in 1664 he in turn was succeeded by his brother, Metacomet, or Philip. The English of Plymouth colony were concerned that the Wampanoag sachems were selling land in the area to English settlers from Providence and other locations outside their colony. They demanded that Philip turn over his people's firearms to the English, that he submit his sachemdom to the authority of the Plymouth government, that he cease selling land to other English, and that he pay a fine. In 1675 a Christian Massachusett Indian named John Sassamon accused Philip of planning for war. Shortly afterward, Sassamon's body was found under the ice of Assawomset Pond near Middleboro, Massachusetts. The English, using this event as a pretext, accused Philip of having ordered Sassamon's death and organized for war against him.

Accounts vary as to who fired the first shot. According to Deputy Governor John Easton of Rhode Island, many of the English who lived near Philip's headquarters at Mount Hope abandoned their homesteads; some Wampanoag looted their houses; and an English youth shot and killed one of the looters. The next day, June 24, 1675, the Wampanoag killed this youth and eight other English settlers and then wounded two more, all in the town of Swansea. The Reverend John Callender of Providence, who wrote a history of Rhode Island and Providence Plantations in 1736, suggested that Philip himself did not desire war.

> There is a constant tradition among the posterity of the [English] people, who lived next to him, and were familiarly conversant with him, as also with the Indians who survived the war, that both Philip and his chief old men were utterly averse to the war, and they show the spot

> (Kikemujit spring. . . . in Bristol) where Philip received news of the first Englishmen that were killed, with grief and sorrow, and wept at the news; and that a day or two before the first outrages, he had protected an Englishman the Indians had captivated, rescued him from them, and privately sent him home safe.

By July 1675, whether they wanted it or not, Philip and his followers were locked in a struggle against the English of Plymouth, Massachusetts Bay, Connecticut, and New Haven.

The Narragansett sachems assured Roger Williams that they had no agreement with Philip to support him against the English. The United Colonies mistrusted the Narragansett, had long coveted their land, and feared that the Narragansett might commit their 1,000 to 2,000 fighting men to Philip's side. Twice in July they sent soldiers to Narragansett country. On the second of these occasions, July 15th, they forced four low-ranking sachems to sign a treaty "as attorneys" for the major sachems Ninigret, Pessacus, Canonchet, Pomham (who had returned to the Narragansett fold), and Quiapen (the Old Queen), even though the minor sachems did not have the authority to represent their superiors. In this treaty the minor sachems promised not to provide shelter to Wampanoag refugees and affirmed that all earlier land deeds with the English were valid. This meant that colonists in Massachusetts and Connecticut would still claim title to the remaining Narragansett country through the discredited Atherton mortgage.

By this time Miantonomi's son Canonchet was the paramount Narragansett sachem. Under duress, he confirmed the July treaty in October during a visit to Boston. He was feeling increasingly abused and humiliated by English suspicion, use of force, and one-sided treaty requirements. He apparently grew reluctant to turn Wampanoag refugees over to English authorities, with good reason. Whether the Wampanoag were hostile or not, Plymouth authorities sold them into slavery in the West Indies. In October 1675, when the English in Massachusetts asked him to surrender the Wampanoag refugees, Canonchet is reported to have given the reply that plunged the Narragansett into King Philip's War: "No," he said, "not a Wampanoag, nor the paring of a Wampanoag's nail."

The 17th century sachem Canonchet is represented today by this stone statue on the common in the town of Narragansett.

The Great Swamp Fight, shown in a 19th-century illustration.

In part because the Narragansett refused to turn over the wounded or fearful Wampanoag who had come to them for sanctuary, the United Colonies declared war on them on November 2, 1675. The colonists believed that Canonchet was preparing to enter the fray on Philip's side and intended to take no chances. Ninigret, the aged sachem of the Niantic, maintained English trust and thereby kept his people out of the developing crisis.

The Narragansett withdrew into a large, hidden, palisaded fort on an island in the Great Swamp in South Kingstown. The English, however, had some intelligence information about their location. On Sunday, December 19, 1675, the army of about 1,000 men from the United Colonies marched across the ice-covered swamp and destroyed the Narragansett sanctuary. The colonists inflicted massive casualties on the Indians and drove the survivors out of their refuge. An account written by Nathaniel Saltonstall of England the following year describes the disaster that would become known to history as the Narragansett Great Swamp Fight.

King Philip, in an engraving copied from one made by the 18th-century American patriot and silversmith Paul Revere. The print was published by Thomas Church, whose father had led the English troops that surprised and killed the Wampanoag chief, ending King Philip's War.

The next day, about noon, they [the colonial troops] come to a large swamp, which by reasons of the frost all the night before, they were capable of going over (which else they could not have done). They forthwith in one body entered the said swamp, and in the midst thereof was a piece of firm land, of about three or four acres of ground, whereon the Indians had built a kind of fort, being palisaded round, and within that a clay wall, as also felled down abundance of trees to lay quite round the said fort, but they had not quite finished the said work. . . . [I]n a short time our forces entered the fort. . . . [A]s soon as ever our men had entered the fort, the Indians fled, our men killed many of them, as also of their wives and children, amongst which an Indian blacksmith (the only man amongst them that fitted their guns and arrow-heads;) and amongst many other houses burnt his, as also demolished his forge. . . . Our men as near as they can judge, may have killed about 600 Indian men, besides women and children.

In the winter and spring of 1676 the remaining Narragansett took revenge. Under Canonchet they carried on guerrilla warfare in Warwick, Seekonk, Rehoboth, and other localities and burned 103 of the 123 houses in Providence. In April a group of English soldiers with Pequot-Mohegan allies captured Canonchet and turned him over to the Indians for execution. When told that he would be executed he replied, "I like it well, I shall die before my heart is soft or I have said anything unworthy of myself." He asked that Uncas's son, the only man of sufficient rank to deserve the honor, be the one to kill him.

In July Connecticut militia killed the Old Queen, the sachem Quiapen, with many of her followers. In August the English captured and executed Quanopen, the sachem who had succeeded Canonchet. An English party under Captain Benjamin Church surprised and killed King Philip at Mount Hope on the morning of August 12, 1676.

King Philip's War was over. The Narragansett country had been ravaged and depopulated. Perhaps fewer than 200 Narragansett survived from a prewar population that was probably between 5,000 and 7,000. Many of the survivors were forced into years of servitude with Rhode Island families and some were sold into slavery in other colonies. Others fled north to Maine and Canada. In the 40-year period between the time Providence was first settled and the end of King Philip's War, the Narragansett had lost their entire territory. In one year English forces had killed or removed more than 95 percent of their population. Looking back at these events of more than three centuries ago, we can only ask whether there could have been a different ending. Could this genocide have been avoided? ▲

Ninigret II as he appeared in 1681, about five years before he became the Narragansett-Niantic sachem. This is believed to be the first portrait painted by a European of an American Indian.

THE RESERVATION PERIOD

Ninigret, the Niantic sachem, had maintained a neutral course between the participants in King Philip's War, and for this reason his people survived in their forested homeland, which was centered around what is now Charlestown, Rhode Island. In the years after the war, a few surviving Narragansett and other New England Indians merged with the Niantic. Whatever their original affiliation, all members of the combined group thus formed were generally referred to as Narragansett. Rhode Island colony assumed jurisdiction over Narragansett and Niantic country after the war. The colony in turn recognized the sachem Ninigret and his heirs as the legal owners of the remaining Niantic-Narragansett land. The population of Ninigret's sachemdom was probably about 500, making it one of the largest enclaves of Indians remaining in southern New England at that time.

Other Narragansett survivors also lived in scattered pockets throughout Rhode Island in Newport, Jamestown, North Kingstown, South Kingstown, East Greenwich, Providence, Warwick, and elsewhere. Little is known of these smaller groups. In most cases they were forced to work as servants for colonists.

Ninigret died of old age near the end of the war. In 1679 his daughter, Weunquesh, was crowned at her fort on Chemunganock Hill in the heart of Niantic territory. She ruled as the Narragansett-Niantic sachem until her death around 1686. She was followed by her half brother, Ninigret II, who ruled until his death in 1723. His reign was long and would be an important one for the tribe, for he was responsible for setting up the reservation that was to be their home for many generations to come.

In 1708 the colony appointed a committee of trustees to negotiate with Ninigret II as to how much land the Narragansett would need for their livelihood. In the decades following King Philip's War, there had been enormous pressure by colonists to move into Nar-

Brass comb or hair fastener, believed to have belonged to Weunquesh, who was the Narragansett-Niantic sachem after her father, Ninigret, and before her brother, Ninigret II.

ragansett-Niantic territory. In 1709 Ninigret II agreed to a quitclaim, ceding to Rhode Island colony all title to Indian land except for a 64-square-mile tract of shoreline, salt pond, farmland, cedar swamp, and woods in Charlestown. By arriving at an agreement with the colony, Ninigret II gave up much Indian land but was successful in obtaining a legal guarantee for the protection of the part of the domain that he retained. He agreed in the deed "never to dispose of the said land or any part thereof, without the free consent of the Governor and Company of Rhode Island." From 1709 until the final sale of the reservation to the state in 1880, the Rhode Island legislature would exercise legal control over the tribe and its affairs.

The sachems were, in effect, executors or legal managers of the large Indian estate and were thus considered under colonial law to have status similar to that of English landed gentry. They received the revenues from their property, paid taxes, and could sue and be sued in the courts. Although the sachems seem to have enjoyed the same rights as white colonial freemen, the other tribal members were not landowners and did not have such rights. The common people were wards of the state. They could live on the reservation property but could not buy or sell the land that they used. They were not citizens and therefore did not vote in town elections. The reservation system did benefit the common people, however, in several ways. They were not asked to pay taxes, they could not easily be held responsible for their debts, and they had a land base for their subsistence where they could live rent free. This land base was important because English planters and small farmers found southern Rhode Island to be an excellent agricultural area and sought to obtain every available acre. By the early 1700s, English planters had established in the area a large number of profitable estates, operated largely by slave labor. The slaves were of African and West Indian origin and included some Caribbean Indians and, after King Philip's War, some nonreservation Narragansett.

The reservation system had a major weakness. In practice the sachem was the sole beneficiary of money raised through the lease, rent, and sale of tribal land to whites. The Rhode Island legislature, through appointed overseers, reviewed the deeds and contracts signed by the sachem. On occasion the legislature nullified transactions to protect the sachem from dishonest persons and sometimes made it difficult for the sachem to sell land. But generally the legislators allowed the sachem to sell land in order to raise funds to repay his personal debts. Thus the sachems were able to live a comfortable existence by selling off the tribal estate.

The English planters who bought the land were often the same persons who extended credit to the sachems. These planters were also influential in the colonial legislature. Why should they prevent the sachem from repaying debts by transferring land to them? It was to their interest, however, to protect the sachem from other creditors. For this reason, as well as to protect the sachems from unscrupulous persons, the legislature established overseers to serve as guardians and manage the sachem's business affairs. Overseers, however, often found ways to obtain Indian land for themselves. The common people of the tribe had free access to the timber, fishing sites, soil, and other resources of the reservation but had no way to stop the sachem from selling these assets to colonists.

Charles Augustus Ninigret succeeded his father in 1723 and held office until his death in 1735. As with other members of the Ninigret family, he identified with the English planter class of the South County area. The Reverend James MacSparran of St. Paul's Episcopal Church in the English town of Narragansett was the most prominent English clergyman among the planters. Charles Ninigret donated a considerable piece of land to King George of England and on it a small structure, known as the Church of England in Charlestown, was built. This church served as a base for the Reverend James MacSparran, who preached there to the English and Narragansett whenever he came to Charlestown. This was the first Christian church to be introduced among the Narragansett. The common people probably did not attend to any significant degree.

Several English colonial observers have left us glimpses of the Narragansett at about this time. Bishop George

Berkeley, a well-known Episcopal clergyman and philosopher, traveled to the Narragansett country in 1729. He received a sad impression of Indian living conditions: "These are either all servants or labourers for the English, who have contributed more to destroy their bodies by the use of strong liquors than by any means to improve their minds or save their souls." The Reverend John Callender of Providence depicted them in equally humble circumstances: "After the war, they were soon reduced to the condition of the laboring poor, without property, hewers of wood and drawers of water." The probate inventory of the estate of Toby Champlin, an elderly Narragansett who died in 1740, contained what the historian William Weeden described as "the humblest sort of an outfit, including scythes, tools, fishing gear, oyster tongs and an old horse."

In the early decades of the 18th century, the Narragansett had become a poor rural folk who struggled to make a living around the edges of the white plantation economy. The sachem's family was an exception. Here, for example, is an account of the household of sachem George Ninigret by Dr. Alexander Hamilton, who visited the sachem's house in Charlestown in 1744. George Ninigret was the brother of Charles Augustus Ninigret. He became the tribal leader when Charles died in 1735 and ruled until his death in 1746.

Upon the road here stands a house belonging to an Indian King named George, commonly called King George's house or palace. He possesses twenty or thirty 1000 acres of very fine level land round this house, upon which he has many tenants and has, of his own, a good stock of horses and other cattle. This

Cloudy Day, Rhode Island, *painted by Martin Johnson Heade in the late 19th century.*

King lives after English mode. His subjects have lost their own government policy and laws and are servants or vassals to the English here. His queen goes in a high modish dress in her silks, hoops, stays, and dresses like an English woman. He educates his children to the belles lettres and is himself a very complaisant mannerly man. We pay'd him a visit, and he treated us with a glass of good wine.

The 1740s marked an important change in the religious life of the Narragansett. At this time a large number (probably the majority) of the reservation community converted to Christianity. In the winter of 1741–42, the first major religious revival in North America, known as the Great Awakening, swept through the English and black populations of southern New England. The preachers in this revival and their followers were known as New Lights because they believed that they had discovered a new and more certain way for the salvation of human souls. The Reverend Joseph Park of Westerly, a Harvard-trained English Congregational minister, organized a New Light church for his English followers from the Westerly-Charlestown area. Early in 1743 a large number of curious Narragansett began attending the services there. Soon many joined Park's church.

According to letters Park wrote at the time, conversion seems to have helped the Narragansett to adapt better to other aspects of colonial life. He noted that the converts drank less al-

St. Paul's Episcopal Church in Narragansett, Rhode Island, as it appeared in the early 19th century. The Reverend James MacSparran, who served as rector of St. Paul's from 1721 until his death in 1757, also preached to colonists and Narragansetts at a small church in Charlestown.

cohol than before, quarreled less, and desired to be educated. He wrote in 1744 that "there is among them a change for good respecting the *outward* as well as the *inward* man. They grow more decent and cleanly in their outward dress, provide better for their households, and get clearer of debt." Park further added, "Ever since the Lord has been graciously among the Indians manifesting his Power and Glory;

Sachem Thomas Ninigret built this house in Charlestown and later sold it and an adjoining farm to an English farmer. His descendants lived in "King Tom's House" (shown in an early- 20th-century photograph) until it burned in 1922.

they have been desirous of a *School* among them, that their children and all such as can, might learn to read. . . . All that we have been able yet to do, is to employ an *Indian Woman* to keep *School* in a *Wigwam*."

The New Light churches were more lively and emotional than the Old Light, or traditional, congregations, but they were less stable. Park's church was no exception. By 1745 an English faction withdrew to set up its own "Separate"

congregation. About this time the Narragansett members also withdrew, under the leadership of the Narragansett Samuel Niles.

Niles, a commoner from the reservation, stood out as a moral person and a capable preacher. Ezra Stiles of Newport once talked with Niles and wrote the following comments in his diary:

> Samuel Niles *cannot read*. It seems extraordinary that such an one should be a Pastor. He is however acquainted with the Doctrines of the Gospel, and an earnest zealous Man, and perhaps does more good to the Indians than any White Man could do. He is of an unblameable Life as to Morals and Sobriety. He had very great Influence over the Indians.

The Reverend Joseph Fish of North Stonington, Connecticut, who also knew Niles, informs us that the Narragansett called him Father Sam. Fish wrote in a letter to a friend in Boston, "This Niles (Who I have known Some Years,) is a Sober Religious Man, of Good Sense and great Fluency of Speech; and know not but a very honest Man. Has a good deal of the Scriptures by heart, and professes a Regard for the Bible." Niles was the first of a long line of Narragansett ministers who served the tribe's Christian members.

In 1750 Niles and his hundred or so Indian followers built a wooden meetinghouse with an adjoining cemetery and open common in the heart of the Charlestown reservation. Niles baptized adults as well as infants whose parents requested it. When any members returned to former sinful practices such as drunkenness, adultery, or stealing, the rest of the congregation mourned for them in church as though the sinners had died. The best-known and most enduring ritual associated with the Narragansett Indian Church is the August Meeting, an annual gathering that probably began during the first years of the church. Its origins, perhaps, go back even further, to the traditional fall harvest ritual.

Sachem George Ninigret died in 1746, and his infant son, Thomas Ninigret, inherited the tribal estate under the guardianship of his mother and with the support of the reservation community. During Thomas Ninigret's reign, from 1746 to 1769, many Narragansett realized fully the implications of the cumulative loss of their land. It became clear to them that if the sachem continued to sell land as his predecessors had, they would not have enough to make a living. The reservation had shrunk so much that any further sales would create impossible land shortages for the common people.

Some form of sachem's council had always existed, and in the mid-1700s it became the advocate for those Narragansett who were threatened by land loss, commoners who were not affiliated with the sachem's family. They petitioned the Rhode Island legislature and were successful to a degree in persuading it to slow down the process.

Thomas Ninigret's reign proved to be the most costly and divisive in the history of the Ninigret family. His relatives paid for their living expenses and his education in England with the rents received from English farmers. As "King Tom" matured, his standard of living and his debts became legendary. Because of the years he had spent in England and his experience living in the style of the rural gentry, Thomas was somewhat of a stranger to his Indian roots.

Under the Reverend Samuel Niles, John Shattock, Tobias Shattock, and others, some of whom were members of the council, the common people of the reservation made an effort to depose the sachem and halt the loss of Indian land. They retained a lawyer, Matthew Robinson, and enlisted two prominent English ministers, Joseph Fish and Eleazar Wheelock, to assist them. In 1768 John and Tobias Shattock even went to England to seek the king's support. In early May, shortly after they arrived, Tobias died of smallpox while they were in Edinburgh, and he was buried there. John returned from England in September without success, apparently unable to see the king or influence him in any way. The sachem continued to sell whatever lands he pleased. When he died, the Rhode Island legislature ordered the sale of even more land to repay his debts.

After Thomas Ninigret's death, Samuel Niles and his group petitioned the Rhode Island legislature to abolish the position of sachem and replace it with a council to be composed mainly of the common people from the reservation. The common people, the legislature, and the sachem's family agreed in 1770 on which lands were to be sold to settle King Tom's debts, and the people agreed to support Thomas's sister Esther, who succeeded him and became queen sachem. By this time the assembly had forbidden any further sales of reservation property.

The tribe, with an Indian honor guard, crowned Esther queen on Coronation Rock in Charlestown in 1770. Unlike her brother, Esther Ninigret had not had an English education. An Englishwoman who knew her said, "Queen Esther was imbued with a

Letter from Mary Secuter to the Reverend Eleazer Wheelock, offering her resignation as teacher at a school for Indians. "I am quite discouraged with myself," she wrote. "I don't think I shall ever do any good to the Cause."

haughty spirit, and could not be induced to speak a word of English, averring that she would never speak the language of the destroyer of her people."

Esther Ninigret died in 1777 of natural causes, and her son, George Sachem, succeeded her. He died in an accident when a tree fell on him around 1779. Although descendants of the Ninigret family live today in the Charlestown-Westerly area, George was the last hereditary Narragansett sachem.

As reservation property passed from Indians to colonists, the residents had to think creatively to find other ways to survive. The Narragansett, together with other poor and dispossessed Connecticut and Long Island Indians, formulated a plan to move to the Oneida Iroquois reservation in central New York State, where open land was still available. The Mohegan Reverend Samson Occum and his son-in-law Joseph Johnson were key figures in planning this move. They persuaded the Oneida sachems to provide them with a tract on their reservation, and this deed was confirmed in 1774. The following year some Narragansett emigrated to the Oneida reservation near Brothertown, New York. The Oneida stipulated in their deed that the land grants "shall not be possessed by any persons deemed of the said Tribes who are descended from or have intermixed with negroes and mulattoes." According to 18th-century records, there had been considerable intermarriage between blacks and Indians in southern

Rhode Island. Clearly the Oneida shared the antiblack prejudice of the white communities around them and, like the whites, considered Indians to have higher status than blacks.

In the 1830s and 1840s the Brothertown Indians, who in addition to Narragansett included Mohegan, Pequot, and Montauk as well as other New England and Long Island people, moved farther west to Brothertown, Wisconsin, near Green Bay, where they established a permanent home. Like many Americans throughout the 19th century, other Narragansett moved even farther west to Michigan, Kansas, North Dakota, and California. Those who stayed behind continued to live on or near the Charlestown reservation.

Following George Sachem's death in 1779, the tribe elected a governor or president and four council officers every year. This system combined post-revolutionary American elective office with traditional forms of leadership. The Rhode Island legislature continued to appoint white overseers, guardians, or their equivalents to supervise tribal affairs.

In 1792 the Rhode Island legislature approved the first Narragansett tribal constitution. This constitution specified voting procedures within the tribe: "All the males of said tribe, of 21 years of age, shall and may meet together at the school house, their accustomed place of meeting, on the last Tuesday in March, A.D. 1792, and annually, and every year on that day, for the purpose of electing their Council, which shall be chosen by

Samson Occum, a Mohegan who led the exodus of New England Indians to the Oneida Reservation in New York State.

a majority of votes, and that in such meetings, and all others, and upon all occasions, every male person of 21 years, born of an Indian woman belonging to said tribe, or begotten by an Indian man belonging thereto, of any other than a negro woman, shall be entitled to vote."

By the late 18th century, most Narragansetts spoke English. Narragansett ceased to be a spoken language around 1810. Nevertheless, particular Indian words and phrases remained in use throughout the 19th century and, to a lesser extent, in the 20th century. Many

The interior of St. Paul's Episcopal Church in Narragansett. Blacks and Indians sat in the balcony, while whites had family pews on the first floor.

Narragansett words persist today as part of our general vocabulary: quahog (hard-shell clam), tautog (a saltwater fish), squaw, wigwam, powwow, sachem, and papoose.

Rule by elected council did not end factionalism and controversy within the reservation community. On several occasions tribal members accused the elected council members of selling land for personal profit. The Rhode Island legislature at times intervened to defuse disputes within the Indian community. In 1849 the tribe approved a new constitution that reaffirmed the five-person elected council (one member of which was to be president). This new consti-

tution also gave the Narragansett greater control over the removal of wood from the Indian Cedar Swamp. It provided for the elderly poor and specified procedures to be followed to keep the schoolhouse in good order.

The occupations and economic situation of the Narragansett in the middle of the 19th century were about the same as that of the poorer working-class whites and blacks who lived in the area. Many tilled small farms, cut wood, or worked as day laborers, carpenters, stonecutters, or stonemasons. Stonemasonry was and still is an important craft of Narragansett men. They built many of the walls, foundations, fireplaces, chimneys, wells, and even mill buildings in southern Rhode Island. In 1859, Narragansett masons constructed the granite church that still stands on the site of the earlier wooden structure in the Charlestown reservation. The number of Narragansett living in Charlestown at this time was about 147. By now, all Narragansett possessed some degree of black and/or white ancestry.

Despite the new constitution and the rebuilt church, the days of the Narragansett reservation were coming to an end. A new idea was beginning to influence state and federal policy toward reservation communities during the last half of the 19th century. The idea was that American Indians could best adapt to U.S. society by giving up what limited protection and support the federal government provided. This viewpoint held that the reservation system and their tribal organization were preventing Indians from becoming fully integrated members of the mainstream American society. Many public figures and political leaders believed that by breaking up tribal relations—disbanding the reservation to allot the land to individuals as private property—and extending U.S. citizenship to tribal members, the government would help American Indians dive into the ethnic "melting pot" on an equal basis with other Americans. At the national level this policy culminated in the General Allotment Act (also known as the Dawes Act) of 1887. By this act, some federal reservations became private in-

Lester Skeesuk, a Narragansett-Mohegan of Brothertown, Wisconsin.

stead of tribal property; the land was subdivided and individual Indians were allotted plots of land on which they were to live and farm.

The idea of making the reservations in their area private property that could be bought and sold had been on the minds of state politicians in Massachusetts, Connecticut, and Rhode Island for some years. As early as 1858 the Rhode Island commissioner of the Narragansett Tribe of Indians had written to the legislature, "It would, no doubt, be better for the tribe and the town, if their condition were changed, and they were placed on an equal footing with other citizens of the State."

The nearby Wampanoag of Mashpee and Gay Head in Massachusetts incorporated as the Town of Mashpee and the Town of Gay Head in 1870. In their cases, what had been state reservations became towns where both Indians and non-Indians could buy and sell land as they wished.

The Rhode Island legislature favored detribalization (ending the tribal status) of the Narragansett but by a different method than that used at Mashpee and Gay Head. The state offered to buy the reservation property from the tribe and then to put the land up for auction. The assembly appointed a board of commissioners to oversee the

(continued on page 73)

Drawing of the home and farm of Henry Marchant in South Kingstown, around 1785. Narragansett men were skilled stonemasons, and they built fences and other structures throughout southern Rhode Island.

MADE BY RHODE ISLAND'S INDIANS

Like other Indian people of New England, the Rhode Island Narragansett fully participate in the contemporary life of their communities. At the same time, however, they are maintaining connections to their past and revitalizing traditions that they hope will live on into the future. Among the most determined to renew the Narragansett cultural heritage are craftspeople who use the techniques and materials of the past to create lovely and useful objects in the present.

Centuries ago, Narragansett women and men made everything they needed from materials they collected in their territory, and traded some of their wares to other Indians in the northeast. When Europeans came to their shores, the Indians traded with them as well, receiving new tools and materials in return. Steel files, glass beads, manufactured cloth and yarn, commercial dyes—these and other equipment led to new and improved designs. Today, Narragansett artisans continue to develop new design ideas and to craft objects that, although unlike those of their prehistoric past, recall the rich heritage of the people who have lived in Rhode Island since earliest times.

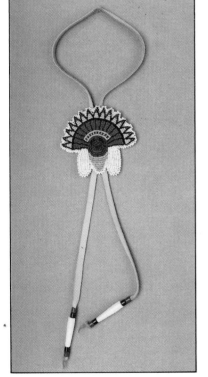

Bola tie of glass beads sewn to leather, showing a stylized man's head wearing a feather bonnet, a design inspired by headdress worn on special occasions by Plains Indians. The ends of the tie are adorned with tile beads and hair pipes. Made by Len Bayrd in 1977.

Earrings made from guinea hen feathers by Len Bayrd in 1981. Bayrd uses natural materials to make ornaments, much like the New England Indians of the past did. These pieces by Bayrd were included in the exhibit We're Still Here: Art of Indian New England, *held at the Children's Museum in Boston in 1987.*

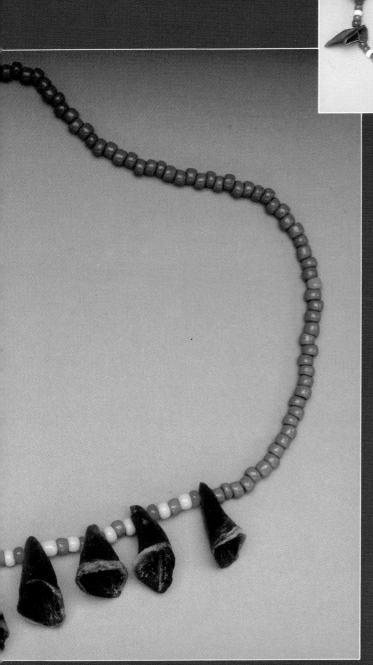

Left: *Necklace of dew claws (small, undeveloped claws) and pony beads on leather thong.* Above: *Necklace of deer hooves and crow beads on leather thong. Bayrd gets the hooves, dew claws, and other animal parts for these necklaces from hunters, cleans them and drills holes in them so they can be strung on long strips of leather.*

67

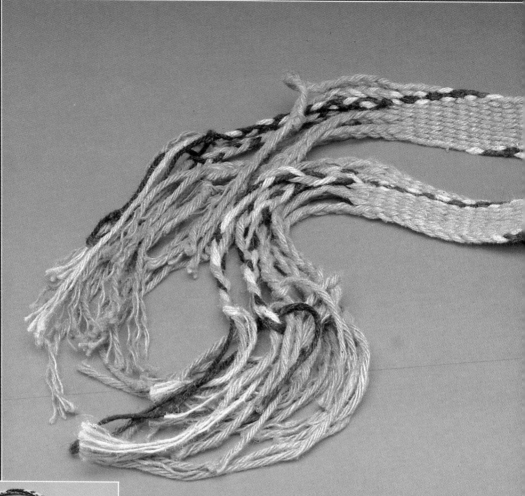

Ella Thomas Sekatau is not only a political activist but also an artisan whose weavings are noted throughout New England. She made the items shown here at Plimouth Plantation in 1977, and they were exhibited at the Children's Museum in Boston in 1987. Above: A finger-woven sash made of hemp colored with natural dyes, 77 inches long by 1 inch wide. Finger-weaving is a technique that does not require a loom; it is similar to, but much more complex than, braiding or plaiting, and can involve numerous strands of cord or yarn. Left: Finger-woven hemp bag with four-directions motif, 6½ inches by 6½ inches.

Bag twined by Ella Thomas
Sekatau of cedar bark and
hemp, with feather and shell
decoration, 7½ inches by
3½ inches. The artist's work
is based on the styles and
designs of similar objects
from the 17th century.

In the 1930s, Princess Red Wing became the leader of efforts to revitalize the Narragansett's sense of their creative past. In the magazine **Red Dawn** she published legends, wrote down oral traditions, and printed illustrations of her people's past, at the same time informing readers of similar efforts being made by Indians throughout North America. Above: Headband made by Princess Red Wing in the traditional fashion—without a loom, and using very fine small beads.

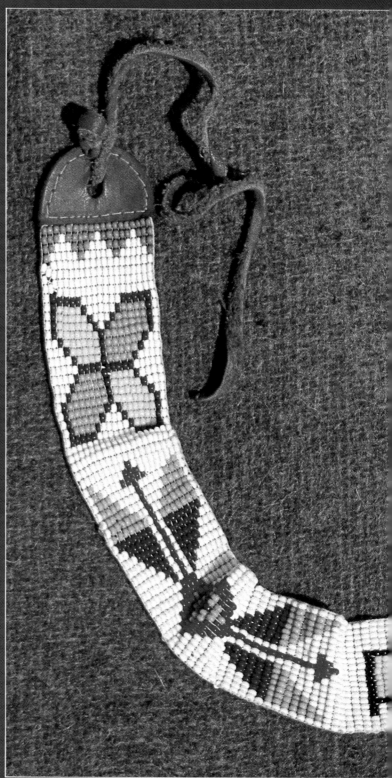

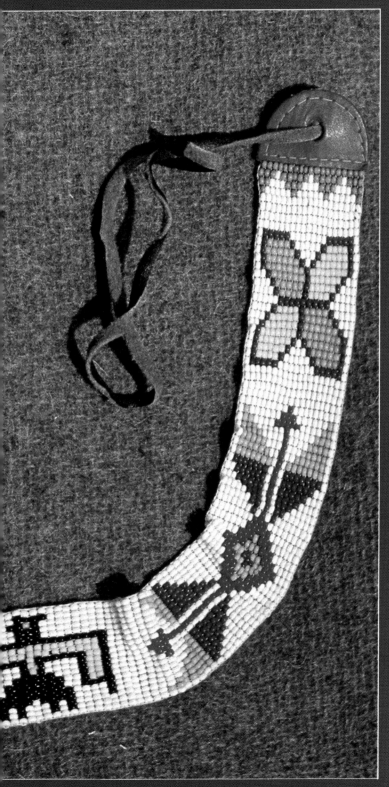

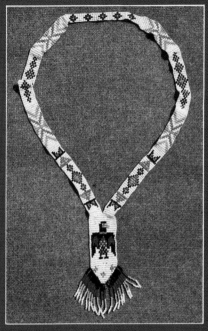

Princess Red Wing studied traditional crafts and taught them to adults as well as children throughout her long life. She made the fine beadwork headband (left) and necklace (above) and wore them daily as symbols of her Indian heritage. Before she died in 1986 in her early 90s, she gave them to a dear friend, with instructions to show them to the Narragansett and other people so that her efforts would live on.

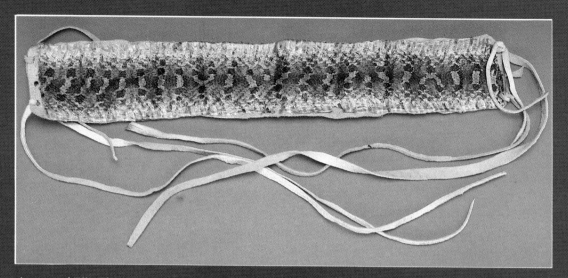

As part of Ella Thomas Sekatau's efforts to perpetuate the traditions of the New England Indians, she uses different types of natural and manufactured materials to create a variety of accessories or regalia. Above: Headband made of rattlesnake skin on leather, 43 inches by 2½ inches including ties.

Headband of rattlesnake skin on leather, embroidered with flattened and twisted porcupine quills and quahog shell disks, 30 inches by 2½ inches.

(continued from page 64)

detribalization procedures. The commissioners kept careful records of their meetings with the tribe, and these records are rich sources of information about the Narragansett in the 1870s.

Many Narragansett opposed detribalization. They liked their distinctive way of life and questioned the value of becoming citizens. Because of racial discrimination by white society, they feared they would lose the security and safeguards they had formerly enjoyed. As far as many whites were concerned, the Narragansett no longer merited being considered Indian because they had acculturated to the general American way of life. They spoke the same language and wore the same clothing as other Americans and had intermarried with both whites and blacks to a considerable extent. Whites simply lumped them together with blacks and all other Indian groups as "colored."

In his statement in opposition to detribalization, Joshua H. Noka, a member of the tribal council, described well the effects of the prejudice of the period:

> For a colored man to be a citizen, he will remain about the same as at the present time. . . . [H]e can't expect ever to be President of the United States, or an Attorney-General. It makes no difference how well he is qualified, he can't be put into a jury box, to be drawn as a common juror, or anything of the kind; but if you have got a cesspool to dig out, put him in there.

Daniel Sekater, another council member, agreed: "It is no use for a man to make a bargain and trade unless it is going to benefit him in some way, and I can't see that citizenship would be worth anything to me." Others spoke of their attachment to the reservation where they and their parents had been born and the bones of their ancestors were buried. The tribe, however, was divided on this issue. Some people resisted detribalization; others endorsed it. The records do not identify which party was in the majority.

The commissioners and the tribe held a series of hearings in 1879. The council agreed to sell the remaining 922 acres to the state of Rhode Island for

Narragansett property in Charleston, 1878.

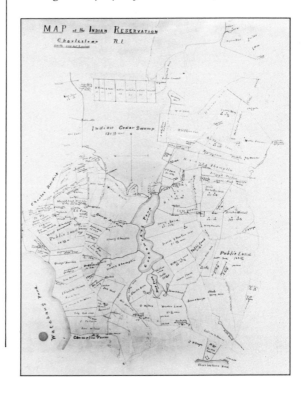

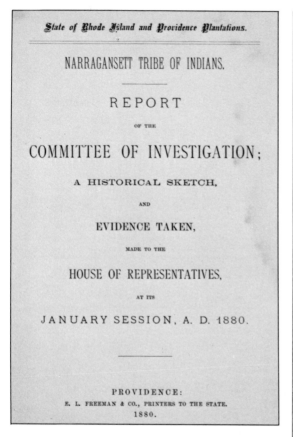

In 1880, the committee appointed by the Rhode Island legislature to study the Narragansett's land holdings published its report.

$5,000 and formally to end tribal relations (the tribe acting as a legal entity for dealing with the state legislature). After a lengthy investigation, the state determined that 324 men, women, and children could claim membership and thus receive a share of the sale. Each individual received $15.43. Most of these people lived in Charlestown, but some lived in Providence and other nearby communities.

The commissioners wrote in their *Third Annual Report* in 1883: "This relation which has existed for nearly two hundred and fifty years is now terminated, and the name of the Narragansett tribe now passes from the statute books of the State."

In 1884 a group of Rhode Island civic and social leaders conducted a ceremony to dedicate Fort Ninigret (the ruins of Ninigret's fort in Charlestown) as a state park. Gideon Ammons, who was president of the last tribal council, spoke on this occasion of the passing of his people: "Our tribe now has no legal existence, and no person can be found to represent the Indian race. The change is so great, I feel sorry to think of it."

That the Narragansett had ceased to exist in the public mind is evident from the 1885 Rhode Island census. This census lists 199 Indians in Rhode Island, but not a single one in Charlestown. The Charlestown town clerk was no longer counting the Narragansett as Indians.

The Rhode Island commissioners and legislature tried to be honest and fair in terminating the reservation and reimbursing members of the tribe for the sale of their land. However, they had, probably unknowingly, violated a key piece of legislation passed by the first United States Congress almost a century earlier. This legislation was the Indian Trade and Intercourse Act of 1790 or, as it is commonly known, the Nonintercourse Act of 1790. President George Washington had interpreted

The State House, Providence, Rhode Island.

this act in a speech to the Seneca Iroquois Nation. His address included the following significant sentences:

> Here then, is the security for the remainder of your lands. No State, no person, can purchase your lands, unless at some public treaty, held under the authority of the United States. . . . When you may find it for your interest to sell any part of your lands, the United States must be present, by their agent, and will be your security that you shall not be defrauded in the bargain you may make.

The Narragansett sale did not conform to the conditions of the Nonintercourse Act. A later generation of Narragansett would make good use of this lapse to change their history in a surprising way. ▲

Sign alongside Route 2 in Charlestown indicates the location of the Narragansett Longhouse.

RESURGENCE
IN THE
MODERN WORLD

The Narragansett community did not disappear after detribalization, the sale of their land, and the end of their relations with the state legislature in 1880. Persons of Narragansett ancestry continued to attend the church and August Meeting, and some form of tribal organization also persisted. People continued to earn their living and provide for their families as they had been doing. They continued to work as stonemasons. Some raised sheep, whose fleece was sold to the textile mills in the area. Like other New Englanders, they grew vegetables and kept pigs, cows, turkeys, and chickens on small family farms. Horse- or ox-drawn carts sufficed for transportation. And Narragansett youngsters attended the same primary schools as other Charlestown children.

The period following detribalization was uneventful, but as the lights of Narragansett identity appeared to flicker, a new consciousness of Indian identity began to surface throughout Indian America. This new consciousness changed the way the Narragansett thought about themselves. Early in the 20th century, they began to have a sense of pan-Indian identity, a recognition that they, as Narragansett, were connected to American Indians elsewhere on the continent. This new appreciation of Indian life and culture was bringing a sense of renewal to Indians across the continent and was even beginning to affect the thinking of American political leaders.

In the 1920s and 1930s, U.S. Indian policy did an about-face. It switched from detribalization to retribalization under the leadership of John Collier, who was commissioner of Indian Affairs in the 1930s. Collier encouraged a climate of respect toward native American traditions. He believed that the Indians should be allowed to choose their own forms of government and the tribal ways by which they wanted to live. Collier's success in changing policy at the national level was reflected in the Indian Reorganization Act (IRA) of 1934. The IRA established the procedures through which a tribe could become recognized by the federal government as an autonomous, self-governing organization.

This reversal in federal policy toward Indian cultures had a direct impact on the Narragansett. By the 1920s they already had joined an intertribal organization of Indians in the northeastern states: the Algonquin Council of Indian Tribes. In 1934 they retribalized as the Narragansett Tribe of Indians, a nonprofit corporation under Rhode Island law. Membership was open only to those persons who could prove that they were direct descendants of people who had been members of the tribe at the time of its dissolution in 1880. Even after it was dissolved, the Narragansett had continued to have sachems and pawwaws. Tribal members expanded the earlier system of an elected president and four council members to one in which they elected a chief sachem and nine council members every other year. According to Chief Sachem Walter Babcock, who was elected in 1988, the chief sachem is customarily elected for life, although his or her name continues to appear on the ballot at each election. The council members are voted for individually. This governing structure is still in effect today.

In 1935 and 1936 a number of Narragansett, under the inspiration of Princess Red Wing, published a monthly magazine that chronicled their tribal re-

birth. Entitled *Narragansett Dawn*, the magazine contained articles by Narragansett on tribal history, oral traditions, social events, recipes, news about other tribes, and much more. For more than half a century, Red Wing was a pioneering spokesperson for the pan-Indian movement, by introducing texts and information about non-Narragansett Indians to her people.

Affiliation with an intertribal Indian organization, the new tribal government, and the monthly magazine all pointed the way to a new direction in Narragansett history. Not only were they emphasizing the value of their own traditions, they were also asserting a larger cross-tribal identity shared with other American Indian groups near and far. People came to use Indian names, such as Lone Wolf, Ishonowa, and Ousamequin, more often. Participants in the August Meeting increasingly wore clothing and hairstyles inspired by early historic-period Indians and especially by western Indians from the Great Plains. In all this the Narragansett were not alone; the pan-Indian movement, begun in the 1920s, continued spreading across the country throughout the 20th century. Other New England Indians, such as the Gay Head and Mashpee Wampanoag, the Connecticut Mohegan, and the Hassanamisco Nipmuck (who live near Worcester, Massachusetts), all plunged into the ethnic Indian revival.

Twentieth-century Indian leaders across North America emphasized two kinds of goals. The first was cultural: a

Wall near Narragansett Bay. Narragansett men continue to work as stonemasons.

renewed pride in being Indian. The second was political: improvement of the Indians' position in the material world of jobs, education, access to government benefits and other resources, and civil rights. In the 1920s progress toward the political goal began for the Narragansett when they took a small step forward and joined with the Wampanoag and others in an intertribal organization. In 1934 they took a second step forward with the decision to retribalize. In the late 1940s they continued on this path, building their own council chambers. The Narragansett Longhouse was constructed at the edge of the old reservation at Charlestown specifically as a place where the political affairs of the tribe could be conducted.

In the late 1960s and the 1970s, there were dramatic and proud assertions of ethnic identity as well as of social and political rights from minority groups throughout the United States. Indian rights activists were among the most

visible. In 1969 a Sioux Indian historian and activist, Vine Deloria, published *Custer Died for Your Sins: An Indian Manifesto*, detailing the biases of white Americans in dealings with Indians. Two years later, in *Of Utmost Good Faith*, Deloria quoted treaties, legal rulings, and other documents showing unjust treatment of Indians by government officials, as well as speeches by contemporary Indian leaders. About this same time, an intertribal group occupied Alcatraz Island in San Francisco Bay as a symbolic attempt to reclaim land that Indians had lost. In New England, the Wampanoag dramatically asserted their political presence at a Thanksgiving Day celebration at Plymouth. These events and others received substantial attention in newspapers and on television and brought American Indian issues before the non-Indian public as they had never been before. These activities also inspired a whole new generation of American Indians. Whereas

Princess Red Wing, photographed when she was in her late eighties. As a young woman in the 1930s she pioneered the renewal of interest in the Narragansett heritage.

the previous generation of Indian leaders had emphasized cultural revival, the younger generation experimented more boldly with political change.

Two Narragansett, Ella Thomas Sekatau and her husband, Eric Thomas Sekatau, are good examples of the transition in Indian leadership that took place in the 1970s. Early in their political careers they had played a major part in reconstructing the 17th-century New England Indian village that is now a permanent component of the large outdoor museum of Pilgrim history at Plimouth Plantation in Massachusetts. The presence of this Indian village alongside the reconstructed English Pil-

grim settlement was a clear announcement to the American public that New England Indians were an essential part of the American past as well as an active part of the present.

Non-Indians began to take notice, and their attitudes changed in response to this new activism. They became more respectful of the Indians' point of view. The town of Jamestown, Rhode Island, for example, returned to the tribe for reburial the large collection of 17th-century Narragansett skeletons that had been excavated at the West Ferry site. The Reverend Harold Mars, minister of the Narragansett Church, officiated at the reburial ceremony. His wife, Laura Mars, sang the Lord's Prayer. The tribal chairman, Chief Sachem George Watson (Chief Red Fox), helped return the bones to the earth from which they had been excavated. Russell Spears, a Narragansett stonemason, built the stone wall that now encloses the reburial site. This was among the earliest instances, and may even have been the first, of human remains being returned to an Indian tribe for reburial. Those who returned the bones asserted that Narragansett graves deserved as much respect as graves of European colonists.

In addition to his contribution to the Indian program at Plimouth Plantation, Eric Thomas Sekatau helped bring about some major political changes. In 1973, as Narragansett tribal coordinator, he represented the tribe at a meeting of eastern American Indians in Washington, D.C. Here is his account of the importance of the meeting:

The Federal Regional council [of New England Indians] and the New England Native Americans . . . were able to call a meeting of all East Coast Native Americans to meet in Washington, D.C., in the summer of 1973. . . . The meeting was one of tremendous significance especially when one realizes that Native Americans from up and down the coast had never met before as a group.

The problems before them were, in Eric Sekatau's words, "how to deal with the issue of land taken from them and to cope with the changes that had come during the years in which their right to govern themselves as Native Americans had eroded."

The Native American Rights Fund (NARF) had been founded a few years earlier to assist Indian groups such as the Narragansett, who could not afford

Harold Mars, center, officiates at a ceremony reburying the skeletal remains that had been removed during an excavation of the 17th century site at West Ferry.

their own legal counsel. NARF was a Colorado-based law firm supported by grants from private foundations and the federal government. It established a team of lawyers to assist native American legal claims across the country. NARF lawyers would advise and represent the Narragansett in their efforts to regain their land.

The Narragansett Tribe of Indians then took steps to recover some of its lost land. On January 8, 1975, the Narragansett filed suit in the U.S. District Court for Rhode Island against the state and against certain non-Indian landowners for 3,200 acres around Charlestown. The tribe claimed that the state of Rhode Island had taken this acreage from it in violation of the Nonintercourse Act of 1790. Still in effect, the 1790 act required the federal government to supervise or approve any trans-

Ellison "Tarzan" Brown (right) after his induction into the Indian Athletic Hall of Fame.

fer of land from "any Indian nation or tribe of Indians." The federal government had had no part in supervising or approving the sale of Narragansett reservation lands in 1880 or earlier.

Federal courts had held that an Indian tribe must demonstrate four points to bring suit:
1. It is or represents an Indian "tribe" within the meaning of the Nonintercourse Act.
2. The parcels of land at issue are covered by the Act as tribal land.
3. The United States has never consented to the transfer of the tribal land.
4. The trust relationship between the United States and the tribe, which is established by coverage of the Act, has never been terminated or abandoned by the United States.

In 1975 the Passamaquoddy tribe of Maine won a landmark case against Secretary of the Interior Rogers C. B. Morton that forced the secretary to recognize the tribe, despite the department's failure to provide the protection of a trust relationship for many years. Had the department provided trust protection to the Passamaquoddy reservation land, the state of Maine would have been unable to take the land whether it had paid for it or not. Following this case, the federal courts determined the criteria for defining a tribe. For legal purposes, a "tribe" was defined as "a body of Indians of the same or similar race, united in a community under one leadership or government and inhabiting a particular, though sometimes ill-defined, territory."

The case of *Passamaquoddy vs. Morton* provided legal precedent for the Narragansett when they made their case against the state of Rhode Island and certain private landowners under the terms of the Rhode Island Indian Claims Settlement Act. The parties to the litigation settled out of court in 1978. Their agreement gave the tribe 1,800 acres of wooded public and private land within the heart of its old domain. The state of Rhode Island then created the Land Management Corporation, to be controlled by the Narragansett, to oversee the management of the newly obtained land. Later that year, the Narragansett completed and submitted a lengthy petition to the U.S. Department of the Interior in which it applied for federal recognition. Ella Thomas Sekatau and Eric Thomas Sekatau had prepared 15 volumes of documents to be submitted in support of this petition. These efforts were successful, and in 1983 the federal government recognized the Narragansett as a tribe. Recognition opened the way for increased federal aid for education, health care, housing, and job training, all of which the tribe has received.

Membership in the modern tribe is limited to persons who can demonstrate descent from any of the 324 Narragansett who participated in the detribalization process in 1880. The core population of Narragansett in the Charlestown area today is about 300 persons. Several hundred more live outside the home area, in Providence and elsewhere. An article in the *Providence Journal* commented on Narragansett life at this time: "The vast majority of Narragansett in Rhode Island live simple, rural, working-class lives that place a great deal of emphasis on as-

Ella Thomas Sekatau, who has led efforts to regain the Narragansett's traditional land.

August Meeting, the Narragansett powwow, has been held annually for hundreds of years. This photograph was taken in front of the Narragansett Indian Church during the 1925 powwow.

sociation with relatives—and most of them are at least distantly related to one another.''

In recent years, rival factions within the tribe have competed spiritedly for elective office in the tribal council and for a voice in allocating the new resources that are available to the tribe. One prominent faction consists of those who consider themselves more traditional, who identify with past Narragansett customs and with the symbols of pan-Indian identity. They trace their roots to those Narragansett who they claim never converted to Christianity. On the other side are those whose attitude seems more pragmatic and who have become more assimilated and more integrated into the non-Indian mainstream society.

Behind these rivalries and symbolic affiliations are long histories of relationships between families that go back many generations and that only an in-

digenous Narragansett can fully understand. A tribal election in 1986, for
example, pitted a traditionalist slate
against a group of candidates headed
by David Mars of Charlestown. Mars,
who ran successfully for chief sachem,
is a descendant of the 18th-century minister Samuel Niles.

The August Meeting still serves to
bring the tribe, including its rival factions, together under the Narragansett
name. A *Providence Journal* reporter visited the 1980 August Meeting after a
major intratribal conflict had been extensively covered by the local newspapers. His comments reveal the ways
in which the August Meeting serves as
a unifying influence.

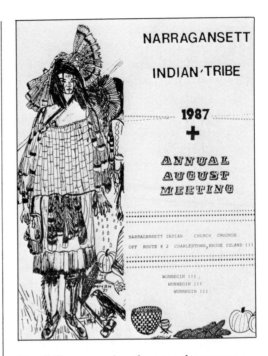

Handbill announcing the annual powwow.

> The annual Narragansett Tribe
> August Meeting is a celebration of
> religion, culture, corn and
> togetherness. That last aspect might
> have been in short supply yesterday
> at the opening of the two-day festival.
> But tribe officials said the recent stir
> . . . was unfelt at the meeting. "I can
> see no effect of it. We are all working
> together," said Chief Sachem Red
> Fox, George Watson. "You have to
> put that behind, here," said Medicine
> Man Running Wolf, Lloyd Wilcox.
> The spirit of the August Meeting
> demands that "nothing is valued
> more than friendship," he said. . . .
> Today's meeting will include two
> religious services at the Narragansett
> Indian Church, one at 10 a.m. and
> another at noon. The services, led by
> the Rev. Harold Mars, will be
> Christian, non-sectarian, Wilcox said.
> All are welcome.

Their 1978 land settlement and the
Narraganett's new status as a federally
recognized tribe have changed their
history in ways that could not have
been easily foreseen. It would appear
that under the terms of the 1978 Rhode
Island Indians Claims Settlement Act
they are still subject to Rhode Island law,
except that through their Land Management Corporation they can establish
their own regulations concerning hunting and fishing on the settlement lands.
Federal recognition, however, also
means that in certain limited ways they
are a separate nation within the United
States. In the late 1980s the tribe applied
to the federal government to have its
land declared an Indian reservation
with standard federal trust protection.

Approval of this application could conceivably increase their independence from state and local control in regulatory matters such as commerce, building, and zoning requirements and marriage licenses, but would probably not alter the state's jurisdiction over criminal and civil matters. For example, the Western, or Mashantucket Pequot, who live across the state line in Connecticut, won federal recognition and trust protection in 1983. The Mashantucket Pequot have regulatory but not civil or criminal jurisdiction within their reservation.

The increasing independence of the Narragansett in the 1980s caused friction between the tribe and the Town of Charlestown. In 1985, over the town's strenuous objections, the state passed legislation that gave the tribe complete ownership of the 1,800 acres that were to have been administered by the Land Management Corporation. They did so in order to make the tribe eligible for federal funds. These tribal trust lands are not subject to property taxes. Town officials worried that the tribe, the town's second largest property owner with about 7 percent of the land, would

The Narragansett Indian Church in Charlestown.

continue to buy or be given acreage. If this happened, the tribe would be removing property from the tax rolls while continuing to make use of the town's police department, schools, and other tax-supported services. The town is challenging the state's 1985 ruling and would like to block the tribe's bid to acquire federal trust status for its land until the jurisdictional issues between tribe and town have been resolved.

The most explosive issue among the Narragansett today is high-stakes bingo. The Western, or Mashantucket Pequot have opened a lucrative and extremely popular bingo operation and restaurant on reservation property. Bingo players come in by chartered bus from miles around. Because their settlement confers regulatory jurisdiction, the Mashantucket Pequot are not bound by state regulations that limit gambling. Some Narragansett would like to open a bingo hall on tribal property. They are aware of the wealth that bingo has brought to the Pequot. But most Charlestown residents, including former chief sachem David Mars and a number of other Narragansett, are opposed to bingo. They fear that it will end the quiet isolation of their rural way of life. In 1986 the tribal council voted against it, recommending other possible routes to economic development.

This economic development is contingent upon the tribe acquiring more land and upon their success in acquiring federal trust status for this land. The issue of bingo could come before the council again in the future. Even if the tribe does support the bingo idea, it remains to be resolved whether the terms of its settlement with the state of Rhode Island and with the federal government will allow it to carry out this project.

Many changes have come to the Narragansett over the last several centuries. Through these changes there have run some continuous threads. Local and family connections, for example, have provided a fabric of continuity. Many of the old Narragansett family names—such as Stanton, Brown, Perry, Wilcox, Hazard, Hopkins, Thomas, and Champlin among others—are very much in evidence. The August Meeting and services at the Narragansett Indian Church provide a sense of closeness with the past. But despite many areas of continuity, the recent changes in the political relationship of the Narragansett to the state and federal governments are sure to have consequences for many years. These changes cannot easily be predicted. Even as changes take place, however, the Narragansett roots sink deeper into the territory of their ancestors. ▲

*View of Ninigret Pond from Fort Ninigret in Charlestown, showing
a corner bastion of the fort with the earthworks and ditch built by the
Narragansett during the Pequot War in the early 17th century.*

PLACES AND STORIES
OF THE
NARRAGANSETT

Reminders of the Narragansett of earlier times can be heard and seen throughout Rhode Island. Many places, for example, bear names that the English colonists learned from the Narragansett. A number of locations that figured in Narragansett history have been identified and are accessible to visitors.

Among the sites that can be seen are the remains of several Narragansett fortifications. The Queen's Fort is a massive arrangement of natural glacial boulders and Indian-built stone walls in North Kingstown, Rhode Island. According to legend, the Old Queen Matantuck had occupied an underground chamber, known as the Queen's Chamber, about 100 feet outside the western perimeter of the fort. In his 1904 book *The Lands of Rhode Island as They were Known to Canounicus and Miantunnomu*, Sidney S. Rider said of the chamber that it "consists of an open space beneath an immense mass of boulder rocks; the tallest men can stand within it; the 'floor' is fine white sand; the entrance is so hidden that six feet away it would never be suspected; the boulders piled above it represent a thickness of fifty or sixty feet." The Queen's Chamber remains hidden to this day; many investigators have searched for it without success. But the stone walls of the Queen's Fort can be seen on top of a hill on Stony Lane, on the North Kingstown–Exeter town line.

Another prominent fort site is Fort Ninigret. Now a state park, it overlooks Ninigret Pond south of the Post Road (Route 1) in Charlestown. Captain John Mason visited the sachem Ninigret in this fort in 1637 on his way to battle with the Pequot at Mystic. He wrote in *A Brief History of the Pequot War*: "On the Wednesday morning, we marched . . . to a place called Nayantick . . . where another of those Narragansett Sachems lived in a fort; it being a frontier to the Pequots." Archaeologists Bert Salwen and Susan Mayer excavated this site around 1970. According to them, "the most prominent feature at Fort Ninigret is a well-defined, rectangular earth and stone embankment with five-sided bastions at three of its four corners. . . . The fort was constructed of long ditches, about one meter [three feet] deep, into which wooden posts were vertically set." The main period of occupation was in the 17th century, when the Niantic used it as a stronghold and trading center. Today one can see the outline of the ditch and earthen embankments very clearly.

The outlines of a rectangular Niantic-Narragansett fort are also visible on a dirt road above a mill pond on Chemunganock Hill in the state-owned Burlingame Management Area in Charlestown. The road runs directly through the middle of the fort, which was another marker on the frontier between Narragansett and Pequot country. Ninigret's daughter Weunquesh lived here and was crowned sachem here after King Philip's War.

The ruins of Pomham's Fort are in Warwick. In 1644 Pomham, the Shawomet sachem, who was a Narragan-

Sketch of 1855 showing the ruins of the Queen's Fort, the stronghold of the Sachem Matantuck.

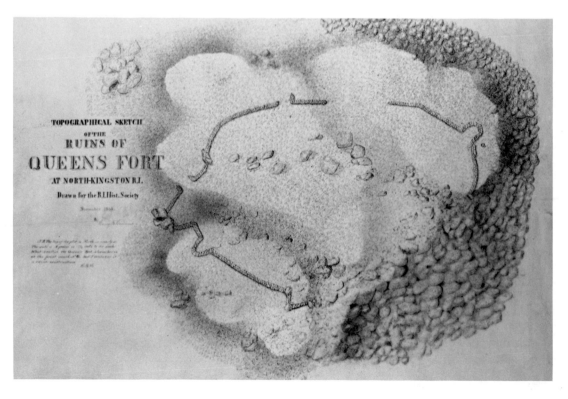

sett subject, declared his independence from the Narragansett sachems and joined with the English of Massachusetts Bay. That colony sent men to Pomham's village near the eastern shore of Warwick Cove, where they built a small palisaded fort for the protection of their new ally. The grass- and brush-covered earthen ramparts of Pomham's Fort can be found in lot 145 on Paine Street in Warwick. The earthworks are in the form of two ovals, one large and one small.

The best-known Narragansett fortification, in the Great Swamp, where the Narragansett defended themselves in King Philip's War, is the hardest to find. People in the area believe that the stone monument marking the site is not where the fight took place. Perhaps the actual battle location still lies undiscovered beneath the soil of that sad and beautiful wilderness. It is also possible, however, that the Great Swamp of the 17th century has partially dried up and is not as extensive today as it was 300 years ago. Thus the fort site may be not in the present-day swamp area but somewhere outside it, under plowed fields. Bullets, spoons, burned corn, and other remains have been found near the perimeter of the swamp, which suggests that this is a possible interpretation.

The old Narragansett reservation area in Charlestown is rich with historic landmarks. The Narragansett Longhouse, built for tribal meetings in the late 1940s, is a small structure, the lower level of a house that has been roofed

Low stones hidden in the grass mark grave sites in the cemetery of the Ninigret family in Charlestown. The tablet was erected by the state of Rhode Island in 1878 "to mark the place which Indian tradition testifies as the Royal Burying Ground of the Narragansett Tribe, and in recognition of the kindness and hospitality of this once powerful Nation to the founders of this State."

over on the west side of Route 2 in Charlestown. Not far away, back in the woods off Old Mill Road, stands the sturdy Narragansett Indian Church, built by Indian masons and stonecutters in 1859. To the rear of this church lies the Narragansett cemetery where the Reverend Samuel Niles was buried in 1785.

(continued on page 94)

NARRAGANSETT NAMES IN RHODE ISLAND

The English settlers of Rhode Island were quick to use the place names used by the Narragansett Indians to identify the sites in their colony. Later Rhode Islanders made abundant use of Narragansett leaders' names for their towns. Here are a few of the Narragansett place names that are in everyday use today.

PLACE NAME	NARRAGANSETT MEANING	LOCATION TODAY
Apponaug	Place where shellfish are roasted	A village in the town of Warwick; Apponaug Cove was an area rich in clams and oysters and where prehistoric Indian shell middens still abound.
Aquidneck	At the island	A large island in Narragansett Bay, now the site of Newport, Middletown, and Portsmouth
Ashaway	Probably, land between the rivers	A village near Westerly
Conanicut	The long place	An island in Narragansett Bay, now the site of Jamestown
Conimicut	Name of the granddaughter of Canonicus, daughter of Queen Quaiapen and the sachem Mixanno	A point of land and a village in Warwick
Coweset	Place of young pines; name of a sachem	Community located between Apponaug and Greenwich

Mashapaug	A large pond or cove	A pond in Providence that was once the site of Narragansett village
Matunuck	High place or observation place	A location on the south shore of Washington Country on Block Island Sound, now best known as a beach area
Meshanticut	Place of big trees	
Moshassuck	Great brook in marshy meadow	A river in Providence
Neutaconcanut	At the short boundary mark	A hill in western Providence
Pawtucket	At the falls in the river	A city north of Providence
Pawtuxet	At the little falls	A village on the border between Cranston and Warwick; also the river that divides the village and these two cities
Potowmut	Low meadow land	A coastal area near East Greenwich
Scituate	At the cold spring or cold brook	A town in central Rhode Island
Shawomet	At the peninsula, or at the neck	A neighborhood in Warwick
Weybosset	Narrow place, forded at low water	The name of a street in Providence
Woonasquatucket	At the head of the tidal river	A river in Providence

Source: John C. Huden,
Indian Place Names of England.
New York: Museum of the American Indian/Heye Foundation, 1962.

The Narragansett Longhouse in Charlestown.

(continued from page 91)

In front of the church extend the open August Meeting grounds. The August Meeting is the oldest and most central ceremonial event of the Narragansett people. The contemporary observance of the August Meeting, also called the Narragansett Powwow, is held annually on the weekend of the second Sunday in August. Large numbers of Narragansett and other nearby Indians come together for the weekend to dance, feast, renew acquaintances, and hold religious services. Those who have moved away to Westerly, Providence, Newport, New Bedford, Boston, and elsewhere come home for this occasion. They come to hear the Narragansett preacher, eat traditional foods such as chowder, sweet corn, clams, and johnnycakes, renew old friendships and kinship ties, and put their feet on Narragansett soil once again.

Cocumpaug Pond, or Schoolhouse Pond, was part of the reservation property. Cocumpaug has been translated as "long pond." The name Schoolhouse Pond originated after the English Congregational minister, the Reverend Joseph Fish, provided funds for the Narragansett to build a school here in the 1760s. A missionary society in Boston, the Society for the Propagation of the Gospel, paid for construction costs and for the teacher's salary. Edward Deake, an Englishman, was the first teacher. He left after several years because of personal difficulties with members of the tribe. He was accused of taking sides in factional disputes, and people were displeased at his admitting white children as well as Indians to the school. Moreover, illness frequently kept him from meeting with his classes. The wooden schoolhouse where he had taught was rebuilt in the 19th century, and it remained standing near the pond until 1968. At that time its non-Indian owners, claiming that it was dilapidated, demolished the building as a safety precaution. In fact, this historic structure could easily have been restored. Many generations of Narragansett children learned their three R's in this school between its beginnings in 1766 and 1880, when it passed from Indian hands.

This whole area in the vicinity of the old reservation, including the Indian Cedar Swamp and the abandoned foundations of many 18th- and 19th-century Narragansett houses, was added to the National Register of Historic Places in 1973. This designation protects the area from highway construction and other forms of development that could destroy these many landmarks of Narragansett history.

The Ninigret family lived near the Post Road but their houses have long since disappeared. They had at least two family cemeteries. The smaller one is on Fort Neck near the site of Ninigret's fort. The other is on a hill north of the Post Road and just north of Hannah Clarkin Pond in Charlestown. Some graves are clearly marked with colonial-style slate headstones. In 1859 a group of Charlestown residents opened one of the graves on Indian Burying Hill and found a collection of En-

Cemetery behind the Narragansett Indian Church on the reservation in Charlestown.

glish trade goods such as brass and iron kettles. Some Narragansett tribal members brought suit against these men for disturbing the grave. Dr. Usher Parsons, a physician who lived in the area, subsequently excavated other graves on

Visitors today can drive along a dirt road to this marker commemorating the Great Swamp Fight, which took place nearby. The pillar records that WITHIN THEIR FORT UPON THIS ISLAND THE NARRAGANSETT INDIANS MADE THEIR LAST STAND IN KING PHILIP'S WAR. The four rocks around the pillar represent the colonies massed against the Indians—Massachusetts, Plymouth, Connecticut, and Rhode Island.

this site. Some of the items found by Parsons are now in the collections of the Peabody Museum at Harvard University and the Rhode Island Historical Society in Providence. Fortunately, these and other Narragansett cemeteries are now protected by law from any person who would disturb the remains.

When a community lives in the same place for many generations, as the Narragansett have lived in Rhode Island since prehistoric time, the past and the present are always in close touch. Children hear stories from their parents and grandparents about people who lived and events that happened long before their birth. These stories float through time and outlive the people who tell them. The Narragansett country is alive with such stories, legends that combine the real with the mysterious. There are legends about local places, about ghosts and devils, and about real people of days gone by. These stories were recorded in the late 19th century and throughout the 20th century. By then, a rich mix of elements of African, European, and Christian origin, as well as some historic episodes, had been incorporated into the legends being told by the Narragansett.

The Crying Rocks in the old reservation in Charlestown are boulders left behind when the North American glacier melted at the end of the last ice age, more than 10,000 years ago. Long ago the Narragansett would leave imperfect babies, born with physical handicaps, in that place. The Narragansett have told stories of people who, passing the

Crying Rocks, heard the wailing of the dead children, at least since the early 18th century. These tales may even pre-date the arrival of Europeans in the area. The Reverend Harold Mars, a carpenter by trade and the retired minister of the Narragansett Indian church, told this version of the story in 1983.

. . . [O]ne of the older Indian men who was a member of the family would tell of passing by these rocks certain hours of the night, late at night, and . . . he would hear what sounded like babies crying and we have heard that story all of our lives and that's how it got its name, the Crying Rocks. Now the story behind that is . . . that the Indians, recognizing the fact that they were exposed to life in the raw so to speak, that when a child was born deformed or crippled in any manner, it was the plan and practice of the Indian people, with proper ceremony, to put that child to death because obviously the child would be handicapped. If he was a man child he would be handicapped as a boy and as a hunter or as a fighter, and so it is said for that reason why they would put the child to death, and this thing having gone on for many years, why there was a build-up of little skeletons, and out of this came the Crying Rocks story. It's been kind of a scary thing, most folks wouldn't go down there [at] two or three o'clock in the morning. . . . This big mass of rocks is located just about . . . a little less than a mile from the church going in a westerly direction down through

The Reverend Harold Mars with his wife Laura and a grandchild.

the woods by the spring . . . on the old reservation right at the edge of the cedar swamp.

Another account of the origin of the Crying Rocks was that the sounds of wailing were those of women and children who had hidden there during the Indian wars in the area. A few miles to the east is Crying Bog, where an Indian mother was said to weep for the children she had abandoned after her white husband deserted her.

Reverend Mars had a rich store of ghost stories related to places in and around Narragansett country. "Many of those kinds of stories," he said, "had

NARRAGANSETT SITES IN CHARLESTON TODAY

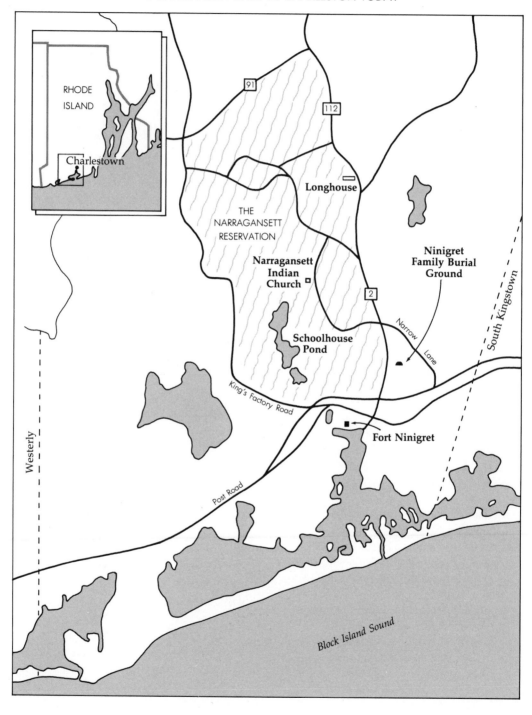

RHODE
ISLAND

Charlestown

91

112

Longhouse

THE
NARRAGANSETT
RESERVATION

Narragansett
Indian
Church

Ninigret
Family Burial
Ground

2

Schoolhouse
Pond

Narrow Lane

South Kingstown

King's Factory Road

Fort Ninigret

Westerly

Post Road

Block Island Sound

to do with dogs barking, chains rattling, and voices crying out at night and groans and things like that—that of course was part of the tradition of our people." Mars told, for example, how a place called Indian Run got its name:

> Indian Run is a little brook that runs side of the old Kingston Road opposite what we call the Old Mountain Field in Peacedale. . . . [T]he ghost story attached to that is the screams of a murdered man. They call it the Indian Run because an Indian man was murdered there and throwed in that brook. . . . [He was killed by a member of the Hazard family, which had migrated into the area.] Many times in land transactions [with whites] if it didn't work out, well, you lost your life. . . . [A]t times they would see blood in the stream.

Non-Indians in the area had a different explanation for the name of Indian Run: In colonial times, Indians had pursued an English settler who had killed one of them, but the Englishman hid in the rocks nearby as the Indians raced past.

Harold Mars believed that some of the ghost stories had been told by elders

> to keep you from trespassing on properties because many times [the colonists] would do bad things to people, they would whip you, or . . . they would take you and send you away [to do forced labor for them]. . . . Many of our people were lost, many things were done; of course, we had no way of documenting these things, no proof to it. . . .

Harold Mars often had a logical or naturalistic explanation for the ghostly sounds or sights of which he spoke. For example, his grandfather had told stories of a headless horse that roamed the area not far from their home. Late one night, when Harold Mars was a youth, he was returning from a Boy Scout meeting

> and as I came up what we call Belmont Avenue in Wakefield, why I was suddenly reminded that that headless horse was just ahead, and true enough, I saw the headless horse, a white horse with no head, and of course I slipped into high gear. And I'll never forget I was so frightened I just fell up against the door at home and broke the door in getting out of the way of the headless horse. But I saw about the next day when I went by there, there was a white horse in a field. . . . [T]hey had low stone walls in that area, and evidently the horse was grazing and I couldn't see his head, I just saw his big body.

Many stories describe competitions between Narragansett men and a stranger who turns out to be the devil. Laura Mars, the wife of Harold Mars, grew up in southern Rhode Island near the old reservation. Her mother told her a story about a man who

> was always playing cards, and [had been told by his family not to do so], but in drinking they got to playing cards this night, and he said he could beat the devil playing cards, so while

he was playing these cards this man came and set down on the other side of the table and begun to play cards with him, and no matter how many games he played, he never could seem to win. And so in the end he gave up, and when he did, this man got up from the table and walked out, and when he did, his feet didn't touch the ground, and he found out he'd been playing with the devil. And from then on he wouldn't play cards any more.

A favorite story concerns a skating contest between a Narragansett named John Onion and a stranger. There is a document recording the baptism of a John Onion in a local Episcopal church on September 24, 1732. This version of the story was told by the late Ferris Babcock Dove, who died in 1983. He had heard the story from his mother who had learned it from her grandmother. Dove, who had owned a restaurant in Rockville, Rhode Island, had been a member of the council and a war chief of the Narragansett tribe.

John Onion was about the fastest skater in the area and he knew it. And he was quite cocky about the whole thing. So this evening he was skating around his friends and everything else. It was just about dusk and he said to his friends, well he says if anybody wants to I'll race up to the other end of the [Cocumpaug or Schoolhouse] pond and back again. And one of the Indians said "You think you're quite good, don't ya?" He said, "Yes, I know I'm good." He said, "Why, I can even beat the devil skating." So with that he took off. Some of the other young fellows started out, but he was so fast he got way ahead of them and in the distance toward the schoolhouse, he happened to see a figure. And he noticed there were sparks coming down where his skates hit the ice. So, and he kept skating towards it. He said "Well, whoever that fellow is, he is really skating cause he's got sparks coming right out of his skates." And when he got up close to him he observed that he had little horns sticking out of his head and not only that, but this fellow as fast as he was going, he just kept skating around him, backwards and cross-toed in front of him and everything else. And John Onion got nervous then, in fact he got scared. And so he hightailed it down the pond, back to Cocumpaug area, to go off to go home. And in the meantime, this little fellow—he skated around him dozens of times on the way down, with his skates, with the sparks coming from his skates. And John Onion realized then that he couldn't of beat the devil, because that had to have been the devil—skating like that, and with that he took off right over the ice, right home with his skates on—didn't bother to take 'em off. And that is the story of John Onion skating against the devil.

Some Narragansett stories have their roots in actual events. Many Narragansett joined American military forces in the American Revolution and the War of 1812. Benny Onion was among those who accompanied Commodore Oliver Hazard Perry against the British in the Battle of Lake Erie in 1813. The encounter has been described by the historian Samuel Eliot Morison in *The Oxford History of the American People* as "a strange naval battle . . . between vessels hastily built of green wood, manned largely by militiamen, Negroes, frontier scouts, and Canadian canal men. The fight was a matter of banging away until one or the other fleet went down; and it was the British that sank." The Perry family lived in southern Rhode Island, and the following story was told by an old Indian woman in 1986 to Edith Townsend, who owned the Commodore Perry Farm in Wakefield.

When Perry's first command [ship] was hit and started to sink, Perry left

Princess Red Wing and other Narragansetts light a ceremonial fire before observing the Strawberry Thanksgiving Festival in 1985 on the grounds of Dovecrest, the restaurant established by the late Ferris Dove and his wife Eleanor. This and other Narragansett thanksgiving festivals (for maple syrup, beans, cranberries, and corn) are celebrated with narrations of the past and present of the Narragansett people, dancing, and feasting.

Clear water bubbles out of a spring to form a brook along a trail on the Narragansett reservation in Charlestown.

in the longboat for the other ship. Benny Onion [was] caught up in the anchor chain on deck [and] called out to [Perry] to save him but Perry did not turn back. Thereupon Onion cursed him and threatened to haunt him forever as he [Onion] went down with the ship. In 1943 no one with Indian blood would stay on his [Perry's] property . . . after dark because Benny Onion walked the

grounds dragging the anchor chain. A mile walk [detour] to Wakefield was preferable [to taking the shorter route through the Perry farm].

Spruce trees, which are abundant in Rhode Island, are said in another story to be the souls of Narragansett who died in colonial wars. The idea that trees can represent the spirits of the departed is probably Indian in origin and may reflect an old Narragansett belief. This story was published in 1936 by Princess Red Wing in the magazine she founded and edited, *Narragansett Dawn*.

One day as a party carried your editor over miles of woodland to find deserted Indianesque spots, an old timer said to her, "You see those stray spruce trees on that hill side?"
"Yes, they look like sentinels."
"They are," said the old timer. "It is said that each of those spruce trees grows where a drop of Narragansett blood was shed. They will ever grow in South County, no matter how much civilization crowds them. It is said of one settler that he decided to cut down every spruce on his 500 acres of Indian land because they haunted him, and he was killed in the attempt. He cut with such vengeance when he heard the story that each spruce was the soul of a Narragansett killed by a white man, that a stately spruce which he set out to destroy fell upon him and killed him."
They really do look, as they stand here, there, and everywhere throughout Narragansett country, that they were souls of departed Red Folk.

A traditional prophecy of the tribes of the eastern United States was described by Eric Thomas Sekatau in 1984.

The oral history of the tribes prophesies that if all land in the Eastern states was lost forever, the end of the world would take place [and] the Turtle who carries the world and humanity on his back [would disappear]. If no one sees the turtle the world is over, for the people of the east are the people of the first light from whom all things are told. [After not being seen for a while] the Turtle returned in the fall of 1978; that year was marked as especially significant in the steps that Eastern native Americans took toward self-determination.

The turtle that returned in the fall of 1978 is in part symbolic of the land that returned to the Narragansett that same year. Much of that land is cedar swamp, where turtles live in great numbers. For now it appears that the turtle and the Narragansett have a secure home, and their world will survive.

We have traveled the entire course of Narragansett existence, from prehistoric time through the colonial period to the present. Once they were the most populous and politically important tribe in southern New England. After the diseases, wars, and other hardships brought upon them by European colonization, very few survived. Those who did come through the colonial bottleneck joined with the eastern Niantic, who had once been Narragansett subjects and who lived nearby in what is now Charlestown and Westerly. The Narragansett of today are descended from this early merging of the Narragansett and Niantic people. They speak English, are American citizens, and live and work like most other Americans. The last people to speak the Narragansett language died early in the 19th century, and the last people of wholly Narragansett-Niantic ancestry died by the middle of that century.

Today's population includes people with black, white, and other Indian in addition to Narragansett-Niantic ancestry. Their shared history, reservation, school, tribal government, church, August Meeting, and oral traditions have helped keep this community alive and distinct over many years. Through changes such as retribalization, the recovery of common land, and their successful petition for federal recognition, the Narragansett people have made a firm claim on their future. Their voice is stronger today than it has been at any point since their defeat in King Philip's War more than three centuries ago. ▲

BIBLIOGRAPHY

Boissevain, Ethel. *The Narragansett People.* Phoenix: Indian Tribal Series, 1975.

Chapin, Howard M. *Sachems of the Narragansetts.* Providence: Rhode Island Historical Society, 1931.

Davis, Hadassah, ed. *What Cheer Netop!: Selections from "A Key into the Language of America."* Providence: Haffenreffer Museum of Anthropology, Brown University, 1986.

Huden, John. *Place Names of New England.* New York: Museum of the American Indian, 1962.

Simmons, William S. *Cautantowwit's House: An Indian Burial Ground on the Island of Conanicut in Narragansett Bay.* Providence: Brown University Press, 1970.

————. "The Narragansett." In *Handbook of North American Indians,* edited by Bruce Trigger. Vol. 15, *Northeast.* Washington, D.C.: Smithsonian Institution, 1978.

————. *Spirit of the New England Tribes: Indian History and Folklore, 1620–1984.* Hanover, NH: University Press of New England, 1986.

Simmons, William S., and Cheryl L. Simmons, eds. *Old Light on Separate Ways: The Narragansett Diary of Joseph Fish, 1765–1776.* Hanover, NH: University Press of New England, 1982.

United States Code Annotated. *Title 25. Indians.* Pocket Supplement. Sections 441–end. St. Paul, MN: West Publishing Co., 1988.

Wilbur, Keith. *New England Indians.* Chester, CT: Globe-Pequot Press, 1978.

Williams, Roger. *A Key into the Language of America.* Includes 4th ed., Narragansett ed., and 5th ed. Reprint (2 vols. in 1). New York: Russell and Russell, 1973.

THE NARRAGANSETT AT A GLANCE

TRIBE *Narragansett*

CULTURE AREA *Narragansett Bay drainage area*

GEOGRAPHY *southern New England*

LINGUISTIC FAMILY *Algonquian*

CURRENT POPULATION *about 300 in the Charlestown, Rhode Island area. About 2,000 total*

FIRST CONTACT *Giovanni de Verrazano, Italian, 1524*

FEDERAL STATUS *recognized*

GLOSSARY

adze A stone implement usually made by grinding rather than chipping and used by prehistoric American Indians for shaping and smoothing timbers.

archaeology The recovery and study of evidence of human ways of life, especially that of prehistoric peoples but also including that of historic peoples.

Archaic Period The period from about 10,000 to 3,000 B.P. when people in North America began using stone and bone tools and obtained food by hunting and gathering. It was generally characterized by seasonal migrations and the use of local natural resources.

B.P. Before the present; years ago.

Cautantowwit The Narragansett creator who lived in the afterworld in the Southwest.

Chepi An Indian spirit that helped pawwaws cause or cure disease.

clan A multigenerational group based on belief in descent from a common ancestor, having a shared identity, organization, and property. Because clan members consider themselves closely related, marriage within the clan is strictly prohibited.

Contact Period The period when Europeans first met Indians in a given area.

culture The learned behavior of human beings; the way of life of a given group of people.

earthworks Any burial mounds, temple mounds, or other large structures built of earth. Most prehistoric earthworks in North America are found on the prairies and in the Eastern Woodlands.

ethnohistory The study of the development of human cultures through archaeological and documentary evidence.

fluted point A type of spear point made by Paleo-Indians; characterized by flutes or grooves made by striking flakes from the base of the point along the side. In the northeastern United States, they date around 12,000–10,000 B.P.

genocide The deliberate destruction of a racial, political, or cultural group.

King Philip's War The major and final war between Indians and English settlers in southern New England, which occurred in 1675–76; named for the Wampanoag chief who died in the war.

manitto Narragansett word for gods or spirits.

mortar A hollow container in which food is pounded or ground by a pestle (see pestle).

Paleo-Indian period The period in North America lasting until about 10,000 years ago, when human culture involved hunting large mammals and making specialized stone tools.

Pan-Indian movement An affirmation of renewed interest in Indian identity that spread throughout North America in the early decades of the 20th century. *Pan*, the Greek word meaning *all*, was used because this movement crossed tribal boundaries, combining cultural features from many tribal traditions into a common sense of Indian identity.

pawwaw Narragansett word meaning medicine man or healer. The derivative word *powwow* has come to mean a ceremonial gathering of Indians.

pestle A club-shaped implement for pounding or grinding substances in a mortar (see mortar).

prehistoric Before written records, or before European contact.

reservation A tract of land set aside by treaty for occupation by and use of Indians. Some reservations were for a single tribe; others were assigned to more than one tribe.

sachem A Narragansett word meaning chief. This was a hereditary title held by both men and women.

sachemdom The people and territory constituting a political unit ruled over by a *sachem*.

technology All of the methods employed by a people to provide the objects necessary for human sustenance and comfort.

textile A woven or knitted cloth.

tradition A distinct way of life, usually restricted to a single region and often lasting for several centuries.

tribe A type of society consisting of several or many separate communities united by kinship, a common culture and language, and such social units as clans, religious organizations and economic and political institutions. The communities making up a tribe are characterized by economic and political equality and thus lack social classes and authoritative chiefs.

wampum Small, cylindrical shell beads made of the purple part of the quahog shell or the white core of the whelk shell. They were used in trade between Indians and Europeans. The purple was worth twice as much as the white.

wigwam A Narragansett dome-shaped house made of poles covered with bark or mats and having a smoke hole at the top.

Woodland period The time when people in North America practiced horticulture, made pottery, used the bow and arrow, buried their dead in cemeteries marked by mounds of earth, and lived in permanent villages. The Eastern Woodland period lasting from about 10,000 to 3,000 years ago.

INDEX

109

PICTURE CREDITS

American Museum of Natural History, pages 24 (Neg. # 1854), 63 (Neg. # 24394); Archaeological Society of Massachusetts, page 27; The Bettmann Archive, pages 39, 50; John Carter Brown Library, page 28; Photos by Kris Craig, Providence Journal Company, pages 80, 83; Dartmouth College Library, pages 60, 61; Photo by John Hopf, page 81; Photos by Bob Kramer, Boston Children's Museum, cover, pages 65–69, 72, 73; Massachusetts Historical Society, page 32; Museum of the American Indian, Heye Foundation, pages 15, 21, 33; Museum of Fine Arts, Boston, page 56; Providence Public Library, page 18; Courtesy of Helen Quattromani, page 101; Rhode Island Historical Society, pages 20, 40, 43, 54, 64, 73, 84, 90; Rhode Island School of Design, Museum of Art, page 53; St. Paul's Church, Committee of Management, page 57; Photos courtesy of William S. Simmons, pages 16, 49, 58, 74, 76, 85, 97; Photo by Charles Thibault, *Westerly Sun*, page 82; Photo by Dr. William A. Turnbaugh, page 22; Photos by Norman Weiser, pages 12, 34, 36, 46, 48, 62, 70, 71, 75, 79, 86, 88, 91, 94, 95, 96, 102; *Westerly Sun*, page 30.

Maps (pages 2, 45, 98) by Gary Tong.

WILLIAM S. SIMMONS is professor and chair of the Department of Anthropology at the University of California, Berkeley. He holds a B.A. from Brown University and an M.A. and Ph.D. from Harvard University. He has done extensive research on the archaeology, ethnohistory, and folklore of southern New England Indians, as well as field research in West Africa and among California Indians. His published Works include *Cautantowwit's House: An Indian Burial Ground on the Island of Conanicut in Narragansett Bay*, and *Old Light on Separate Ways: The Narragansett Diary of Joseph Fish, 1765–1776*, which he coedited with Cheryl L. Simmons.

FRANK W. PORTER III, general editor of INDIANS OF NORTH AMERICA, is director of the Chelsea House Foundation for American Indian Studies. He holds a B.A., M.A., and Ph.D. from the University of Maryland. He has done extensive research concerning the Indians of Maryland and Delaware and is the author of numerous articles on their history, archaeology, geography, and ethnography. He was formerly director of the Maryland Commission on Indian Affairs and American Indian Research and Resource Institute, Gettysburg, Pennsylvania, and he has received grants from the Delaware Humanities Forum, the Maryland Committee for the Humanities, the Ford Foundation, and the National Endowment for the Humanities, among others. Dr. Porter is the author of *The Bureau of Indian Affairs* in the Chelsea House KNOW YOUR GOVERNMENT series.